Two Scottish Tales of Medical Compassion

Two Scottish Tales of Medical Compassion

Rab and his Friends
JOHN BROWN, M.D.

A Doctor of the Old School
IAN MACLAREN

With

A Brief History of the Edinburgh School of Medicine
JOHN RAFFENSPERGER, M.D.

COSIMO CLASSICS

NEW YORK

Two Scottish Tales of Medical Compassion: Rab and his Friends & A Doctor of the Old School, with A Brief History of the Edinburgh School of Medicine. Introduction and "A Brief History of the Edinburgh School of Medicine" copyright © 2011 by John Raffensperger, M.D. "Rab and his Friends" first published by Ticknor & Fields in 1859; this version by David Douglas in 1883. "A Doctor of the Old School" first published by Dodd, Mead & Company in 1895. Current editions published by Cosimo Classics in 2011.

Cover copyright © 2011 by Cosimo, Inc. Cover and interior design © www.popshop-studio.com.

ISBN: 978-1-61640-544-1

Ordering Information:
Cosimo publications are available at online bookstores. They may also be purchased for educational, business, or promotional use:
Bulk orders: Special discounts are available on bulk orders for reading groups, organizations, businesses, and others.
Custom-label orders: We offer selected books with your customized cover or logo of choice.

For more information, contact us at:

Cosimo, Inc.
P.O. Box 416, Old Chelsea Station
New York, NY 10011

info@cosimobooks.com

or visit us at:
www.cosimobooks.com

CONTENTS

INTRODUCTION

THESE TWO TRUE SHORT STORIES, "RAB AND HIS Friends" and "A Doctor of the Old School," should be required reading for every aspiring doctor. Periodic rereading by mature physicians will remind us that compassion and kindness are the cornerstones of our profession.

The main event in "Rab" was an operation performed in 1830 by James Syme, who later became the mentor and father-in-law of Joseph Lister, the man who discovered antisepsis and banished surgical infections. Author John Brown, Syme, and Lister all worked together at the Edinburgh School of Medicine.

"A Doctor of the Old School" vividly portrays a country physician who practiced in the Scottish Highland. He was compassionate, dedicated, and honest; all qualities which reflect Edinburgh teaching.

These two short stories illustrate aspects of medical education, scientific achievement, and the humanistic approach to medicine which made the Edinburgh School the most distinguished English-speaking medical center of the nineteenth century.

—John Raffensperger, M.D., 2011
A Brief History of the Edingburgh School of Medicine

Rab and his Friends

JOHN BROWN, M.D.

PREFACE

FOUR YEARS AGO, MY UNCLE, THE REV. DR. SMITH OF Biggar, asked me to give a lecture in my native village, the shrewd little capital of the Upper Ward. I never lectured before; I have no turn for it; but *Avunculus* was urgent, and I had an odd sort of desire to say something to these strong-brained, primitive people of my youth, who were boys and girls when I left them. I could think of nothing to give them. At last I said to myself, "I'll tell them Ailie's story." I had often told it to myself; indeed it came on me at intervals almost painfully, as if demanding to be told, as if I heard Rab whining at the door to get in our out,—

"Whispering how meek and gentle he could be;"

or as if James was entreating me on his deathbed to tell all the world what his Ailie was. But it was easier said than done. I tried it over and over, in vain. At last, after a happy dinner at Hanley—why are the dinners always happy at Hanley?—and a drive home alone through

"The gleam, the shadow, and the peace supreme"

of a midsummer night, I sat down about twelve and rose at four, having finished it. I slunk off to bed, satisfied and cold. I don't think I made almost any changes in it. I read it to the Biggar folk in the school-house, very frightened, and felt I was reading it ill, and their honest faces intimated as much in the affectionate puzzled looks. I gave it on my return home, to some friends, who liked the story; and the first idea was to print it, as now, with illustrations, on the principle of Rogers' joke, "that it would be dished excepted for the plates."

My willing and gifted friends, Lady Trevelyan, Mrs. Blackburn, George Harvey, and Noel Paton, made sketches, all of which, except Lady Trevelyan's, are given now—her expressive drawing of the carrier on his way home

3

across the snow, being unsuitable, from my words having led her astray as to the locality. Her sketch was of a bleak, open country, and you saw, quite small but full of expression, the miserable man urging the amazed Jess along the muffled road—the smallness of the family party, and the knowledge of what was concentrated there, the sleeping, cold, uncaring expanse of nature made it quick with pathetic life.

But I got afraid of the public, and paused. Meanwhile, some good friend said Rab might be thrown in among the other idle hours, and so he was; and it is a great pleasure to me to think how many new friends he got.

I was at Biggar the other day, and some of the good folks told me, with a grave smile peculiar to that region, that when Rab came to them in print he was so good, that they wouldn't believe he was the same Rab I had delivered in the school-room—a testimony to my vocal powers of impressing the multitude somewhat conclusive.

I like to think that the children's hear so delicately rendered by Mr. Lumb Stocks have among them my dear friend the artist's *Parvula* and my own; I must not say how long it was ago. I need not add that this little story is, in all essentials, true, though, if I were Shakspeare, it might be curious to point out where phantasy tried her hand, sometimes where least suspected.

It has been objected to it as a work of art, that there is too much pain; and many have said to me, with some bitterness, "Why did you make me suffer so?" But I think of my father's answer when I told him this, "And why shouldn't they suffer? *She* suffered; it will do them good; for pity, the genuine pity, is, as old Aristotle says, 'of power to purge the mind.' " And though in all works of art there should be a *plus* of delectation, the ultimate overcoming of evil and sorrow by good and joy—the end of all art being pleasure,—whatsoever things are lovely first, and things that are true and of good report afterwards in their turn—still there is a pleasure, one of the strangest and strongest in our nature, in imaginative suffering with and for others,—

> "In the soothing thoughts that spring
> Out of human suffering;"

for sympathy is worth nothing, is, indeed, not itself, unless it has in it somewhat of personal pain. It is the hereafter that gives to

... "the touch of a vanish'd hand,
And the sound of a voice that is still,"

its own infinite meaning. Our hears and our understandings follow Ailie and her "ain man" into that world where there is no pain, where no one says, "I am sick." What is all the philosophy of Cicero, the wailing of Catullus, and the gloomy playfulness of Horace's variations on "let us eat and drink," with its terrific "for,"—to the simple faith of the carrier and his wife in "I am the Resurrection and the Life."

I think I can hear from across the fields of sleep and other years, Ailie's sweet, dim, wandering voice trying to say—

Our bonnie bairn's there, John,
She was baith gude and fair, John,
And we grudged her sair, John,
     To the land o' the leal.
But sorrow's sel' wears past, John,
The joys are comin' fast, John,
The joys that aye shall last, John,
     Lin the land o' the leal.

Edinburgh, 1861

I

FOUR-AND-THIRTY YEARS AGO, BOB AINSLIE AND I WERE coming up Infirmary Street from the High School, our heads together, and our arms intertwisted, as only lovers and boys know how, or why.

When we got to the top of the street, and turned north, we espied a crowd at the Tron Church. "A dog-fight!" shouted Bob, and was off; and so was I, both of us all but praying that it might not be over before we got up! And is not this boy-nature? And human nature too? And don't we all wish a house on fire not to be out before we see it? Dogs like fighting; old Isaac says they "delight" in it, and for the best of all reasons; and boys are not cruel because they like to see the fight. They see three of the great cardinal virtues of dog or man—courage, endurance, and skill—in intense action. This is very different from a love of making dogs fight, and enjoying, and aggravating, and making gain by their pluck. A boy—be he ever so fond himself of fighting—if he be a good boy, hates and despises all this, but he would have run off with Bob and me fast enough: it is a natural, and not a wicked interest, that all boys and men have in witnessing intense energy in action.

Does any curious and finely ignorant woman wish to know how Bob's eye at a glance announced a dog-fight to his brain? He did not, he could not, see the dogs fighting: it was a flash of an inference, a rapid induction. The crowd round a couple of dogs fighting is a crowd masculine mainly, with an occasional active, compassionate woman fluttering wildly round the outside and using her tongue and her hands freely upon the men, as so many "brutes"; it is a crowd annular, compact, and mobile; a crowd centripetal, having its eyes and its heads all bent downwards and inwards, to one common focus.

Well, Bob and I are up, and find it is not over: a small thoroughbred white bull terrier is busy throttling a large shepherd's dog, unaccustomed to war, but not to be trifled with. They are hard at it; the scientific little fellow doing his work in great style, his pastoral enemy fighting wildly, but with the sharpest of teeth and a great courage. Science and breeding, however, soon had their own; the Game Chicken, as the premature Bob called him, working his way up, took his final grip of poor Yarrow's throat, and he lay gasping and done for. His master, a brown, handsome, big young shepherd from Tweedsmuir, would have liked to have knocked down any man, would "drink up Esil, or eat a crocodile," for that part, if he had a chance: it was no use kicking the little dog; that would only make him hold the closer. Many were the means shouted out in mouthfuls, of the best possible ways of ending it. "Water!" but there was none near, and many cried for it who might have got it from the well at Blackfriar's Wynd. "Bite the tail!" and a large, vague, benevolent, middle-aged man, more desirous than wise, with some struggle got the bushy end of Yarrow's tail into his ample mouth, and bit it with all his might. This was more than enough for the much-enduring, much perspiring shepherd, who, with a gleam of joy over his broad visage, delivered a terrific facer upon our large, vague, benevolent, middle-aged friend—who went down like a shot.

Still the Chicken holds; death not far off. "Snuff! a pinch of snuff!" observed a calm, highly dressed young buck, with an eye-glass in his eye. "Snuff, indeed!" growled the angry crowd, affronted and glaring. "Snuff! a pinch of snuff!" again observes the buck, but with more urgency; whereon were produced several open boxes, and from a mull which may have been at Culloden he took a pinch, knelt down, and presented it to the nose of the Chicken. The laws of physiology and of snuff take their course; the Chicken sneezes, and Yarrow is free!

The young pastoral giant stalks off with Yarrow in his arms,—comforting him.

But the bull terrier's blood is up, and his soul unsatisfied; he grips the first dog he meets, and discovering she is not a dog, in Homeric phrase, he makes a brief sort of *amende*, and is off. The boys, with Bob and me at their head, are after him: down Niddry Street he goes, bent on mischief; up the Cowgate like an arrow—Bob and I, and our small men, panting behind.

There, under the single arch of the South Bridge, is a huge mastiff, sauntering down the middle of the causeway, as if with his hands in his pockets: he is old, grey, brindled, as big as a little Highland bull, and has the Shakespearian dewlaps shaking as he goes.

The Chicken makes straight at him, and fastens on this throat. To our astonishment the great creature does nothing but stand still, hold himself up, and roar—yes, roar; a long serious, remonstrative roar. How is this? Bob and I are up to them. *He is muzzled!* The bailies had proclaimed a general muzzling, and his master, studying strength and economy mainly, had encompassed his huge jaws in a home-made apparatus constructed out of the leather of some ancient *breechin*. His mouth was open as far as it could; his lips curled up in a rage—a sort of terrible grin; his teeth gleaming, ready, from out the darkness; the strap across his mouth tense as a bow string; his whole frame stiff with indignation and surprise; his roar asking us all around: "Did you ever see the like of this?" He looked a stature of anger and astonishment done in Aberdeen granite.

We soon had a crowd; the Chicken held on. "A knife!" cried Bob; and a cobbler gave him his knife: you know the kind of knife, worn away obliquely to a point, and always keen. I put its edge to the tense leather; it ran before it; and then!—one sudden jerk of that enormous head, a sort of dirty mist about his mouth, no noise,—and the bright and fierce little fellow is dropped, limp and dead. A solemn pause; this was more than any of us had bargained for. I turned the little fellow over, and saw he was quite dead; the mastiff had taken him by the small of the back like a rat and broken it.

He looked down at his victim appeased, ashamed, and amazed, snuffed him all over, stared at him, and, taking a sudden thought, turned round and trotted off. Bob took the dead dog up, and said: "John, we'll bury him after tea." "Yes," said I, and was off after the mastiff. He made up the Cowgate at a rapid swing; he had forgotten some engagement. He turned up the Candlemaker Row, and stopped at the Harrow Inn.

There was a carrier's cart ready to start, and a keen, thin, impatient, blackavized little man, his hand at his grey horse's head, looking about angrily for something. "Rab, ye thief!" said he, aiming a kick at my great friend, who drew cringing up, and, avoiding the heavy shoe with more agility than dignity, and watching his master's eye, slunk dismayed under the cart—his ears down, and as much as he had of tail down too.

What a man this must be—thought I—to whom my tremendous hero turns tail! The carrier saw the muzzle hanging, cut and useless, from his neck, and I eagerly told him the story, which Bob and I always thought, and still think, Homer, or King David, or Sir Walter, alone were worthy to rehearse. The severe little man was mitigated, and condescended to say: "Rab, ma man, puir Rabbie!" —whereupon the stump of a tail rose up, the ears were cocked, the eyes filled, and were comforted; the two friends were reconciled. "Hupp!" and a stroke of the whip were given to Jess; and off went the three.

Bob and I buried the Game Chicken that night (we had not much of a tea) in the back-green of his house, in Melville Street, No. 17, with considerable gravity and silence; and being at the time in the Iliad, and, like all boys, Trojans, we called him Hector, of course.

II

SIX YEARS HAVE PASSED,—A LONG TIME FOR A BOY AND A dog: Bob Ainslie is off to the wars; I am a medical student, and clerk at Minto House Hospital.

Rab I saw almost every week, on the Wednesday; and we had much pleasant intimacy. I found the way to his heart by frequent scratching of his huge head, and an occasional bone. When I did not notice him, he would plant himself straight before me, and stand wagging that bud of a tail, and looking up, with his head a little to the one side. His master I occasionally saw; he used to call me "Maister John," but was laconic as any Spartan.

One fine October afternoon, I was leaving the hospital, when I saw the large gate open, and in walked Rab, with that great and easy saunter of his. He looked as if taking general possession of the place; like the Duke of Wellington entering a subdued city, satiated with victory and peace. After him came Jess, now white from age, with her cart, and in it a woman carefully wrapped up, the carrier leading the horse anxiously, and looking back. When he saw me, James (for his name was James Noble) made a curt and grotesque "boo," and said: "Maister John, this is the mistress; she's got a trouble in her breast—some kind o' an income, we're thinkin'."

By this time I saw the woman's face; she was sitting on a sack filled with straw, her husband's plaid round her, and his big coat, with its large white buttons, over her feet.

I never saw a more unforgettable face—pale, serious, *lonely*, delicate, sweet, without being at all what we call fine. She looked sixty, and had on a mutch, white as snow, with its black ribbon; her silvery, smooth hair setting off her dark-grey eyes—eyes such as one sees only twice or thrice in a lifetime, full of suffering, full also of the overcoming of it; her eyebrows black and delicate, and her mouth firm, patient, and contented, which few mouths ever are.

As I have said, I never saw a more beautiful countenance, or one more subdued to settled quiet. "Ailie," said James, "This is Maister John, the young doctor; Rab's freend, ye ken. We often speak aboot you, doctor." She smiled, and made a movement, but said nothing, and prepared to come down, putting her plaid aside and rising. Had Solomon, in all his glory, been handing down the Queen of Sheba at his palace gate, he could not have

11

done it more daintily, more tenderly, more like a gentleman, than did James the Howgate carrier, when he lifted down Ailie his wife.

The contrast of his small, swarthy, weather-beaten, keen, worldly face to hers—pale, subdued, and beautiful—was something wonderful. Rab looked on concerned and puzzled, but ready for anything that might turn up,—were it to strangle the nurse, the porter, or even me. Ailie and he seemed great friends.

"As I was sayin', she's got a kind o' trouble in her breest, doctor; wull ye tak' a look at it?" We walked into the consulting-room, all four, Rab grim and comic, willing to be happy and confidential if cause could be shown, willing also to be the reverse on the same terms. Ailie sat down, undid her open gown and her lawn handkerchief round her neck, and, without a word, showed me her right breast. I looked at and examined it carefully,—she and James watching me, and Rab eyeing all three. What could I say? There it was, that had once been so soft, so shapely, so white, so gracious and bountiful, so "full of all blessed conditions," —hard as a stone, a centre of horrid pain, making that pale face, with its grey, lucid, reasonable eyes, and its sweet resolved mouth, express the full measure of suffering overcome. Why was that gentle, modest, sweet woman, clean and lovable, condemned by God to bear such a burden?

I got her away to bed. "May Rab and me bide?" said James. "*You* may; and Rab, if he will behave himself." "I'se warrant he's do that, doctor"; and in slunk the faithful beast. I wish you could have seen him. There are no such dogs now. He belonged to a lost tribe. As I have said, he was brindled, and grey like Rubislaw granite; his hair short, hard, and close, like a lion's; his body thick-set, like a little bull—a sort of compressed Hercules of a dog. He must have been ninety pounds' weight, at the least; he had a large blunt head; his muzzle black as night, his mouth blacker than any night, a tooth or two—being all he had—gleaming out of his jaws of darkness. His head was scarred with the record of old wounds, a sort of series of fields of battle all over it; one eye out, one ear cropped as close as was Archbishop Leighton's father's' the remaining eye had the power of two; and above it, and in constant communication with it, was a tattered rag of an ear, which was for ever unfurling itself, like an old flag; and then that bud of a tail, about one inch long—if it could in any sense be said to be long, being as broad as long, the mobility, the instantaneousness of that bud were very funny and surprising, and its expressive twinklings and winkings, the intercommunications between the eye, the ear, and it, were of the oddest and swiftest.

Rab had the dignity and simplicity of great size; and having fought his way all along the road to absolute supremacy, he was as mighty in his own line as Julius Caesar or the Duke of Wellington, and had the gravity of all great fighters.

You must have observed the likeness of certain men to certain animals, and of certain dogs to men. Now, I never looked at Rab without thinking of the great Baptist preacher, Andrew Fuller. The same large, heavy, menacing, combative, somber, honest countenance, the same deep inevitable eye, the same look,—as of thunder asleep, but ready,—neither a dog nor a man to be trifled with.

Next day, my master, the surgeon, examined Ailie. There was no doubt it must kill her, and soon. It could be removed—it might never return—it would give her speedy relief—she should have it done. She curtsied, looked at James, and said, "When?" "Tomorrow," said the kind surgeon—a man of few words. She and James and Rab and I retired. I noticed the he and she spoke little, but seemed to anticipate everything in each other.

The following day, at noon, the students came in, hurrying up the great stair. At the first landing-place, on a small well-known blackboard, was a bit of paper fastened by wafers, and many remains of old wafers beside it. On the paper were the words,— "An operation today. J. B., *Clerk.*"

Up ran the youths, eager to secure good places; in they crowded, full of interest and talk. "What's the case?" "Which side is it?"

Don't think them heartless; they are neither better nor worse than you or I; they get over their professional horrors, and into their proper work; and in them pity—as an *emotion,* ending in itself or at best in tears and a long-drawn breath, lessens, while pity, as a *motive,* is quickened, and gains power and purpose. It is well for poor human nature that it is so.

The operating theatre is crowded; much talk and fun, and all the cordiality and stir of youth. The surgeon with his staff of assistants is there. In comes Ailie: one look at her quiets and abates the eager students. That beautiful old woman is too much for them; they sit down, and are dumb, and gaze at her. These rough boys feel the power of her presence. She walks in quickly, but without haste; dressed in her mutch, her neckerchief, her white dimity short gown, her black bombazine petticoat, showing her white worsted stockings and her carpet shoes. Behind her was James with Rab. James sat down in the distance, and took that huge and noble head between his knees. Rab looked perplexed and dangerous; for ever cocking his ear and dropping it as fast.

Ailie stepped up on a seat, and laid herself on the table, as her friend the surgeon told her; arranged herself, gave a rapid look at James, shut her eyes, rested herself on me, and took my hand. The operation was at once begun; it was necessarily slow; and chloroform—one of God's best gifts to His suffering children—was then unknown. The surgeon did his work. The pale face showed its pain, but was still and silent. Rab's soul was working within him; he saw that something strange was going on,— blood flowing from his mistress, and she suffering; his ragged ear was up, and importunate; he growled and gave now and then a sharp impatient yelp; he would have liked to have done something to that man. But James had him firm, and gave him a glower from time to time, and an intimation of a possible kick;—all the better for James, it kept his eye and mind off Ailie.

It is over: she is dressed, steps gently and decently down from the table, looks for James; then, turning to the surgeon and the students, she curtsies,—and in a low, clear voice begs their pardon if she has behaved ill. The students—all of us—wept like children; the surgeon happed her up carefully,—and, resting on James and me, Ailie went to her room, Rab following. We put her to bed. James took off his heavy shoes, crammed with tickets, heel-capped and toe-capped, and put them carefully under the table, saying: "Maister John, I'm for nane o' yer strynge nurse bodies for Ailie. I'll be her nurse, and I'll gang aboot on my stockin' soles as canny as pussy." And so he did; and handy and clever and swift and tender as any woman was that horny-handed, snell, peremptory little man. Everything she got he gave her: he seldom slept; and often I saw his small shrewd eyes out of the darkness, fixed on her. As before, they spoke little.

Rab behaved well, never moving, showing us how meek and gentle he could be, and occasionally, in his sleep, letting us know that he was demolishing some adversary. He took a walk with me every day, generally to the Candlemaker Row; but he was somber and mild, declined doing battle, though some fit cases offered, and indeed submitted to sundry indignities, and was always very ready to turn, and came faster back, and trotted up the stair with much lightness, and went straight to that door.

Jess, the mare, had been sent, with her weather-worn cart, to Howgate, and had doubtless her own dim and placid meditations and confusions on the absence of her master and Rab and her unnatural freedom from the road and her cart.

For some days Ailie did well. The wound healed "by the first intention;" for, as James said, "Oor Ailie's skin's ower clean to beil." The students came in quiet and anxious, and surrounded her bed. She said she liked to see their young, honest faces. The surgeon dressed her, and spoke to her in his own short kind way, pitying her through his eyes, Rab and James outside the circle,—Rab being now reconciled, and even cordial, and having made up his mind that as yet nobody required worrying, but, as you may suppose, *semper paratus*.

So far well; but four days after the operation my patient had a sudden and long shivering, a "groosin'," as she called it. I saw her soon after; her eyes were too bright, her cheek coloured; she was restless, and ashamed of being so; the balance was lost; mischief had begun. On looking at the wound, a blush of red told the secret: her pulse was rapid, her breathing anxious and quick; she wasn't herself, as she said, and was vexed at her restlessness. We tried what we could. James did everything, was everywhere; never in the way, never out of it; Rab subsided under the table into a dark place, and was motionless, all but his eye, which followed everyone. Ailie got worse; began to wander in her mind, gently; was more demonstrative in her ways to James, rapid in her questions and sharp at times. He was vexed, and said: "She was never that way afore; no, never." For a time she knew her head was wrong, and was always asking our pardon—the dear, gentle old woman; then delirium set in strong, without pause. Her brain gave way, and then came that terrible spectacle,

> "The intellectual power, through words and things,
> Went sounding on a dim and perilous way;"

she sang bits of old songs and Psalms, stopping suddenly, mingling the Psalms of David, and the diviner words of the Son and Lord, with homely odds and ends and scraps of ballads.

Nothing more touching, or in a sense more strangely beautiful, did

I ever witness. Her tremulous, rapid, affectionate, eager Scotch voice,—the swift, aimless, bewildered mind, the baffled utterance, the bright and perilous eye, some wild words, some household cares, something for James, the names of the dead, Rab called rapidly and in a "fremyt" voice, and he starting up, surprised, and slinking off as if he were to blame somehow, or had been dreaming he heard. Many eager questions and beseechings which James and I could make nothing of, and on which she seemed to set her all and then sink back ununderstood. It was very sad, but better than many things that are not called sad. James hovered about, put out and miserable, but active and exact as ever; read to her, when there was a lull, short bits from the Psalms, prose and metre, chanting the latter in his own rude and serious way, showing great knowledge of the fit words, bearing up like a man, and doting over her as his "ain Ailie," "Ailie, ma woman!" "Ma ain bonnie wee dawtie!"

The end was drawing on: the golden bowl was breaking; the silver cord was fast being loosed; that *animula blandula, vagula, hospes, comesque*, was about to flee. The body and the soul—companions for sixty years—were being sundered, and taking leave. She was walking, alone, through the valley of that shadow into which one day we must all enter,—and yet she was not alone, for we know whose rod and staff were comforting her.

One night she had fallen quiet, and, as we hoped, asleep; her eyes were shut. We put down the gas, and sat watching her. Suddenly she sat up in bed, and, taking a bed-gown which was lying on it rolled up, she held it eagerly to her breast,—to the right side. We could see her eyes bright with a surprising tenderness and joy, bending over this bundle of clothes. She held it as a woman holds her sucking child; opening out her night-gown impatiently, and holding it close, and brooding over it, and murmuring foolish little words, as over one whom his mother comforteth, and who sucks and is satisfied. It was pitiful and strange to see her wasted dying look, keen and yet vague—her immense love.

"Preserve me!" groaned James, giving way. And then she rocked backward and forward, as if to make it sleep, hushing it, and wasting on it her infinite fondness. "Wae's me, doctor! I declare she's thinkin' it's that bairn." "What bairn?" "The only bairn we ever had; our wee Mysie, and she's in the Kingdom for forty years and mair." It was plainly true: the pain in the breast, telling its urgent story to a bewildered, ruined brain, was misread and mistaken; it suggested to her the uneasiness of a breast full of milk, and then the child, and so again once more they were together, and she had her ain wee Mysie in her bosom.

This was the close. She sank rapidly: the delirium left her; but, as she whispered, she was "clean silly"; it was the lightening before the final darkness. After having for some time lain still—her eyes shut, she said: "James!" He came close to her, and, lifting up her calm, clear, beautiful eyes, she gave him a long look, turned to me kindly but shortly, looked for Rab but could not see him, then turned to her husband again, as if she would never leave off looking, shut her eyes, and composed herself. She lay for some time breathing quick, and passed away so gently that, when we thought she was gone, James, in his old-fashioned way, held the mirror to her face. After a long pause, one small spot of dimness was breathed out; it vanished away, and never returned, leaving the blank clear darkness without a stain. "What is our life? It is even a vapour, that appeareth for a little time, and then vanisheth away."

Rab all this time had been fully awake and motionless; he came forward beside us. Ailie's hand, which James had held, was hanging down: it was soaked with his tears. Rab licked it all over carefully, looked at her, and returned to his place under the table.

James and I sat, I don't know how long, but for some time,—saying nothing: he started up abruptly, and with some noise went to the table, and, putting his right fore and middle fingers each into a shoe, pulled them out, and put them on, breaking one of the leather latchets, and muttering in anger: "I never did the like o' that afore!"

I believe he never did; nor after either. "Rab!" he said, roughly, and pointing with his thumb to the bottom of the bed. Rab leaped up, and settled himself, his head and eye to the dead face. "Maister John, ye'll wait for me," said the carrier; and disappeared in the darkness, thundering downstairs in his heavy shoes. I ran to a front window; there he was, already round the house, and out at the gate, fleeing like a shadow.

I was afraid about him, and yet not afraid; so I sat down beside Rab, and, being wearied, fell asleep. I awoke from a sudden noise outside. It was November, and there had been a heavy fall of snow. Rab was *in status quo;* he heard the noise too, and plainly knew it, but never moved. I looked out; and there, at the gate, in the dim morning—for the sun was not up, was

Jess and the cart,—a cloud of steam rising from the old mare. I did not see James; he was already at the door, and came up the stairs and met me. It was less than three hours since he left, and he must have posted out—who knows how?—to Howgate, full nine miles off, yoked Jess, and driven her astonished into town. He had an armful of blankets, and was streaming with perspiration. He nodded to me, spread out on the floor two pairs of clean old blankets having at their corners "A. G., 1794" in large letters in red worsted. These were the initials of Alison Graeme, and James may have looked in at her from without—himself unseen but not unthought of—when he was "wat, wat, and weary," and, after having walked many a mile over the hills, may have seen her sitting, while "a' the lave were sleepin'," and by the firelight working her name on the blankets for her ain James's bed.

He motioned Rab down, and, taking his wife in his arms, laid her in the blankets and wrapped her carefully and firmly up, leaving the face uncovered; and then, lifting her, he nodded again sharply to me, and, with a resolved but utterly miserable face, strode along the passage, and downstairs, followed by Rab. I followed with a light; but he didn't need it. I went out, holding stupidly the candle in my hand in the calm frosty air; we were soon at the gate. I could have helped him, but I saw he was not to be meddled with, and he was strong and did not need it. He laid her down as tenderly, as safely, as he had lifted her out ten days before—as tenderly as when he had her first in his arms when she was only "A. G."—sorted her, leaving that beautiful sealed face open to the heavens; and then, taking Jess by the head, he moved away. He did not notice me; neither did Rab, who presided behind the cart.

I stood till they passed through the long shadow of the College and turned up Nicolson Street. I heard the solitary cart sound through the streets and die away and come again; and I returned, thinking of that company going up Libberton Brae, then along Roslin Muir, the morning light touching the Pentlands and making them like onlooking ghosts, then down the hill through Auchindinny woods, past "haunted Woodhouselee;" and as daybreak came sweeping up the bleak Lammermuirs, and fell on his own door, the company would stop, and James would take the key, and lift Ailie up again, laying her on her own bed, and, having put Jess up, would return with Rab and shut the door.

James buried his wife, with his neighbours mourning, Rab watching the proceedings from a distance. It was snow, and that black ragged hole would look strange in the midst of the swelling spotless cushion of white. James looked after everything; then rather suddenly fell ill, and took to bed; was insensible when the doctor came, and soon died. A sort of low fever was prevailing in the village, and his want of sleep, his exhaustion, and his misery made him apt to take it. The grave was not difficult to reopen. A fresh fall of snow had again made all things white and smooth; Rab once more looked on, and slunk home to the stable.

And what of Rab? I asked for him next week of the new carrier who got the goodwill of James's business and was now master of Jess and her cart. "How's Rab?" He put me off, and said, rather rudely, "What's *your* business wi' the dowg?" I was not to be so put off. "Where's Rab?" He, getting confused and red, and intermeddling with his hair, said: " 'Deed, sir, Rab's deid." "Dead! What did he die of?" "Weel, sir," said he, getting redder, "he didna exactly dee; he was killed. I had to brain him wi' a rack-pin; there was nae doin' wi' him. He lay in the treviss wi' the mear, and wadna come oot. I tempit him wi' kail and meat, but he wad tak' naething, and keepit me fra feedin' the beast, and he was aye gur-gurrin', and grup-gruppin' me by the legs. I was laith to mak' awa wi' the auld dowg, his like wasna atween this and Thornhill—but, 'deed, sir, I could do naething else." I believed him. Fit end for Rab, quick and complete. His teeth and his friends gone, why should he keep the peace and be civil?

He was buried in the braeface, near the burn, the children of the village, his companions, who used to make very free with him and sit on his ample stomach as he lay half asleep at the door in the sun—watching the solemnity.

A Doctor
of the Old
School

IAN MACLAREN

CONTENTS

PREFACE

IT IS WITH GREAT GOOD WILL THAT I WRITE THIS SHORT preface to the edition of "A Doctor of the Old School" (which has been illustrated by Mr. Gordon after an admirable and understanding fashion) because there are two things that I should like to say to my readers, being also my friends.

One, is to answer a question that has been often and fairly asked. Was there ever any doctor so self-forgetful and so utterly Christian as William MacLure? To which I am proud to reply, on my conscience: Not one man, but many in Scotland and in the South country. I will dare to prophecy also across the sea.

It has been one man's good fortune to know four country doctors, not one of whom as without his faults—Weelum was not perfect—but who, each one, might have sat for my hero. Three are now resting from their labors, and the fourth, if he ever should see these lines, would never identify himself.

Then I desire to thank my readers, and chiefly the medical profession for the reception given to the Doctor of Drumtochty.

For many years I have desired to pay some tribute to a class whose service to the community was known to every countryman, but after the tale had gone forth my heart failed. For it might have been despised for the little grace of letters in the style and because of the outward roughness of the man. But neither his biographer nor his circumstances have been able to obscure MacLure who has himself won all honest hearts, and received afresh the recognition of his more distinguished brethren. From all parts of the English-speaking world letters have come in commendation of Weelum MacLure, and many were from doctors who had received new courage. It is surely more honor than a new writer could ever have deserved to receive the approbation of a profession whose charity puts us all to shame.

May I take this first opportunity to declare how deeply my heart has been touched by the favor shown to a simple book by the American people, and to express my hope that one day it may be given me to see you face to face.

Ian Maclaren.

Liverpool, Oct. 4, 1895

I

A GENERAL PRACTITIONER

DRUMTOCHTY WAS ACCUSTOMED TO BREAK EVERY LAW of health, except wholesome food and fresh air, and yet had reduced the Psalmist's farthest limit to an average life-rate. Our men had made no difference in their clothes for summer or winter, Drumsheugh and one or two of the larger farmers condescending to a topcoat on Sabbath, as a penalty of their position, and without regard to temperature. They wore their blacks at a funeral, refusing to cover them with anything, out of respect to the deceased, and standing longest in the kirkyard when the north wind was blowing across a hundred miles of snow. If the rain was pouring at the Junction, then Drumtochty stood two minutes longer through sheer native dourness till each man had a cascade from the tail of his coat, and hazarded the suggestion, half-way to Kildrummie, that it had been "a bit scrowie," a "scrowie" being as far short of a "shoor" as a "shoor" fell below "weet."

This sustained defiance of the elements provoked occasional judgments in the shape of a "hoast" (cough), and the head of the house was then exhorted by his women folk to "change his feet" if he had happened to walk through a burn on his way home, and was pestered generally with sanitary precautions. It is right to add that the gudeman treated such advice with contempt, regarding it as suitable for the effeminacy of towns, but not seriously intended for Drumtochty. Sandy Stewart "napped" stones on the road in his shirt sleeves, wet or fair, summer and winter, till he was persuaded to retire from active duty at eighty-five, and he spent ten years more in regretting his hastiness and criticizing his successor. The ordinary course of life, with fine air and contented minds, was to do a full share of work till seventy, and then to look after "orra" jobs well into the eighties, and to "slip away" within sight of ninety. Persons above ninety were understood to be acquitting themselves with credit, and assumed airs of authority, brushing aside the opinions of seventy as immature, and confirming their conclusions with illustrations drawn from the end of last century.

When Hillocks' brother so far forgot himself as to "slip awa" at sixty, that worthy man was scandalized, and offered laboured explanations at the "beerial."

"It's an awfu' business ony wy ye look at it, an' a sair trial tae us a'. A' never heard tell o' sic a thing in oor family afore, an' it's no easy accoontin' for't.

"The gudewife was sayin' he wes never the same sin' a weet nicht he lost himsel on the muir and slept below a bush; but that that's neither here nor there. A'm thinkin' he sappit his constitution thae twa years he wes grieve aboot England. That wes thirty years syne, but ye're never the same aifter thae foreign climates."

Drumtochty listened patiently to Hillocks' apologia, but was not satisfied.

"It's clean havers aboot the muir. Losh keep's, we've a' sleepit oot and never been a hair the waur.

"A' admit that England micht hae dune the job; it's no cannie stravagin' yon wy frae place tae place, but Drums never complained tae me as if he hed been nippit in the Sooth."

The parish had, in fact, lost confidence in Drums after his wayward experiment with a potato-digging machine, which turned out a lamentable failure, and his premature departure confirmed our vague impression of his character.

"He's awa noo," Drumsheugh summed up, after opinion had time to form; "an' there were waur fouk than Drums, but there's nae doot he wes a wee flichty."

When illness had the audacity to attack a Drumtochty man, it was describes as a "whup," and was treated by the men with a fine negligence. Hillocks was sitting in the Post Office one afternoon when I looked in for my letters, and the right side of his face was blazing red. His subject of discourse was the prospects of the turnip "breer," but he casually explained that he was waiting for medical advice.

"The gudewife is keepin' up a ding-dong frae mornin' til nicht aboot ma face, and a'm fair deaved (deafened), so a'm watchin' for MacLure tae get a bottle as he comes wast: yon's him noo."

The doctor made his diagnosis from horseback on sight, and stated the result with that admirable clearness which endeared him to Drumtochty.

"Confoond ye, Hillocks, what are ye ploiterin' aboot here for in the weet wi' a face like a boiled beet? Div ye no ken that ye've a titch o' the rose (erysipelas), and ocht tae be in the hoose? Gae hame wi' ye afore a' leave the bit, and send a haflin for some medicine. Ye donnerd idiot, are ye ettlin tae follow Drums afore yir time?" And the medical attendant of Drumtochty continued his invective till Hillocks started, and still pursued his retreating figure with medical directions of a simple and practical character.

"A'm watchin', and peety ye if ye pit aff time. Keep yir bed the mornin', and dinna show yir face in the fields till a' see ye. A'll gie ye a cry on Monday—sic an auld fule—but there's no ane o' them tae mind anither in the hale pairish."

Hillocks' wife informed the kirkyaird that the doctor "gied the gudeman and awfu' clearin'," and that Hillocks "wes keepin' the hoose," which meant that the patient had tea breakfast, and at that time was wandering about the farm buildings in an easy undress with his head in a plaid.

It was impossible for a doctor to earn even the most modest competence from a people of such scandalous health, and so MacLure had annexed neighbouring parishes. His house—little more than a cottage—stood on the roadside among the pines towards the head of our Glen, and from this base of operations he dominated the wild glen that broke the wall of the Grampians above Drumtochty—where the snow drifts were twelve feet deep in winter, and the only way of passage at times was the channel of the river—and the moorland district westwards till he came to the Dunleith sphere of influence, where there were four doctors and a hydropathic. Drumtochty in its length, which was eight miles, and its breadth, which was four, lay in his hand; besides a glen behind, unknown to the world, which in the night time he visited at the risk of life, for the way thereto was across the big moor with its peat holes and treacherous bogs. And he held the land eastwards towards Muirtown so far as Geordie, the Drumtochty post, traveled every day, and could carry word that the doctor was wanted. He did his best for the need of every man, woman, and child in this wild, straggling district, year in, year out, in the snow and in the heat, in the dark and in the light, without rest, and without holiday for forty years.

One horse could not do the work of this man, but we liked best to see him on his old white mare, who died the week after her master, and the passing of the two did our hearts good. It was not that he rode beautifully, for he broke every cannon of art, flying with his arms, stooping till he seemed to be speaking into Jess's ears, and rising in the saddle beyond all necessity. But he could ride faster, stay longer in the saddle, and had a firmer grip with his knees than anyone I ever met, and it was all for mercy's sake. When the reapers in harvest time saw a figure whirling past in a cloud of dust, or the family at the foot of Glen Urtach, gathered round the fire on a winter's night, heard the rattle of a horse's hoofs on the road, or the shepherds, out after the sheep, traced a black speck moving across the snow to the upper glen, they knew it was the doctor, and, without being conscious of it, wished him God speed.

Before and behind his saddle were strapped the instruments and medicines the doctor might want, for he never knew what was before him. There were no specialists in Drumtochty, so this man had to do everything as best he could, and as quickly. He was chest doctor and doctor for every other organ as well; he was accoucheur and surgeon; he was oculist and aurist; he was dentist and chloroformist, besides being chemist and druggist. It was often told how he was far up Glen Urtach when the feeders of the threshing mill caught young Burnbrae, and how he stopped only to change horses at his house, and galloped all the way to Burnbrae, and flung himself off his horse and amputated the arm, and saved the lad's life.

"You wud hae thocht that every meenut was an hour," said Jamie Soutar, who had been at the threshing, "an' a'll never forget the puir lad lying as white as deith on the floor o' the loft, wi' is head on a sheaf, an' Burnbrae haudin' the bandage ticht an' prayin' a' the while, and the mither greetin' in the corner.

" 'Will he never come?' she cries, an' a' heard the soond o' the horse's feet on the road a mile awa in the frosty air.

" 'The Lord be praised!' said Burnbrae, and a' slippit doon the ladder as the doctor came skelpin' intae the close, the foam fleein' frae his horse's mooth.

" 'Whar is he?' wes a' that passed his lips, an' in five meenuts he hed him on the feedin' board, and wes at his wark—sic wark, neeburs—but he did it weel. An' ae thing a' thocht rael thochtfu' o' him: he first sent aff the laddie's mither tae get a bed ready.

" 'Noo that's feenished, and his constitution 'ill dae the rest,' and he carried the lad doon the ladder in his airms like a bairn, and laid him in his bed, and waits aside him till he wes sleepin', and then says he: 'Burnbrae, yir a gey lad never tae say "Collie, will ye lick?" for a' hevna tasted meat for saxteen hoors.'

"It was michty tae see him come intae the yaird that day, neeburs; the verra look o' him wes victory."

Jaimie's cynicism slipped off in the enthusiasm of this reminiscence, and he expressed the feeling of Drumtochty. No one sent for MacLure save in great straits, and the sight of him put courage in sinking hearts. But this was not by the grace of his appearance, or the advantage of a good bedside manner. A tall, gaunt, loosely made man, without an ounce of superfluous flesh on his body, his face burned a dark brick colour by constant exposure to the weather, red hair and beard turning grey, honest blue eyes that looked you ever in the face, huge hands with wrist bones like the shank of a ham, and a voice that hurled his salutations across two fields, he suggested the moor rather than the drawing-room. But what a clever hand it was in an operation, as delicate as a woman's, and what a kindly voice it was in the humble room where the shepherd's wife was weeping by her man's bedside. He was "ill pitten thegither" to begin with, but many of his physical defects were the penalties of his work, and endeared him to the Glen. That ugly scar that cut into his right eyebrow and gave him such a sinister expression, was got one night Jess slipped on the ice and laid him insensible eight miles from home. His limp marked the big snowstorm in the fifties, when his horse missed the road in Glen Urtach, and they rolled together in a drift. MacLure escaped with a broken leg and the fracture of three ribs, but he never walked like other men again. He could not swing himself into the saddle without making two attempts and holding Jess's mane. Neither can you "warstle" through the peat bogs and snow drifts for forty winters without a touch of rheumatism. But they were honourable scars, and for such risks of life, men get the Victoria Cross in other fields.

MacLure got nothing but the secret affection of the Glen, which knew that none had ever done one-tenth as much for it as this ungainly, twisted, battered figure, and I have seen a Drumtochty face soften at the sight of MacLure limping to his horse.

Mr. Hopps earned the ill-will of the Glen for ever by criticizing the doctor's dress, but indeed it would have filled any townsman with amazement. Black he wore once a year, on Sacrament Sunday, and, if possible, at a funeral; topcoat or waterproof never. His jacket and waistcoat were rough homespun of Glen Urtach wool, which threw off the wet like a duck's back, and below he was clad in shepherd's tartan trousers, which disappeared into unpolished riding boots. His shirt was grey flannel, and he was uncertain about a collar, but certain as to a tie which he never had, his beard doing it instead, and his hat was soft felt of four colours and seven different shapes. His point of distinction in dress was the trousers, and they were the subject of unending speculation.

"Some threep that he's worn thae eedentical pair the last twenty year, an' a' mind masel him getting' a tear ahint, when he was crossin' oor palin', and the mend's still veesible.

"Ithers declare 'at he's got a wab o' claith, and hes a new pair made in Muirtown aince in the twa year maybe, and keeps them in the garden till the new look wears aff.

"For ma ain pairt," Soutar used to declare, "a' canna mak up my mind, but there's ae thing sure, the Glen wud not like tae see him withoot them: it wud be a shock tae confidence. There's no muckle o' the check left, but ye can aye tell it, and when ye see thae breeks comin' in ye ken that if human pooer can save yir bairn's life it 'ill be dune."

The confidence of the Glen—and tributary states—was unbounded, and rested partly on long experience of the doctor's resources, and partly on his hereditary connection.

"His father was here afore him," Mrs. MacFadyen used to explain; "atween them they've hed the countryside for weel on tae a century; if MacLure disna understand oor constitution, wha dis, a' wud like tae ask?"

For Drumtochty had its own constitution and a special throat disease, as became a parish which was quite self-contained between the woods and the hills, and not dependent on the lowlands either for its diseases or its doctors.

"He's a skilly man, Doctor MacLure," continued my friend Mrs. MacFadyen, whose judgment on sermons or anything else was seldom at fault; "an' a kind-hearted, though o' coorse he hes his faults like us a', an' he disna tribble the Kirk often.

"He aye can tell what's wrang wi a body, an' maistly he can put ye richt, and there's nae new-fangled wys wi' him: a blister for the outside an' Epsom salts for the inside dis his wark, and they say there's no an herb on the hills he disna ken.

"If we're tae dee, we're tae dee; an' if we're tae live, we're tae live," concluded Elspeth, with sound Calvinistic logic; "but a'll say this for the doctor, that whether yir tae live or dee, he can aye keep up a shairp moisture on the skin.

"But he's no verra ceevil gin ye bring him when there's naethin' wrang," and Mrs. MacFadyen's face reflected another of Mr. Hopps' misadventures of which Hillocks held the copyright.

"Hopps' laddie ate grosarts (gooseberries) till they hed to sit up a' nicht wi' him, an' naethin' wud do but they maun hae the doctor an' he writes 'immediately' on a slip o' paper.

"Weel, MacLure had been awa a' nicht wi' a shepherd's wife Dunleith wy, and he comes here withoot drawin' bridle, mud up tae the een.

" 'What's a dae here, Hillocks?' he cries; 'it's no accident, is't?' and when he got aff his horse he cud hardly stand wi' stiffness and tire.

" 'It's nane o' us, doctor; it's Hopps' laddie; he's been eatin' ower mony berries.'

"If he didna turn on me like a tiger.

" 'Div ye mean tae say——'

" 'Weesht, weesht,' an' I tried tae quiet him, for Hopps wes comin' oot.

" 'Well, doctor,' begins he, as brisk as a magpie, 'you're here at last; there's no hurry with you Scotchmen. My boy has been sick all night, and I've never had one wink of sleep. You might have come a little quicker, that's all I've got to say.'

" 'We've mair tae dae in Drumtochty than attend tae every bairn that hes a sair stomach,' and a' saw MacLure wes roosed.

" 'I'm astonished to hear you speak. Our doctor at home always says to Mrs. 'Opps, "Look on me as a family friend, Mrs. 'Opps, and send for me though it be only a headache." '

" 'He'd be mair sparin' o' his offers if he hed four and twenty mile tae look aifter. There's naethin' wrang wi' yir laddie but greed. Gie him a gude dose o' castor oil and stop his meat for a day, an he 'ill be a' richt the morn.'

" 'He 'ill not take castor oil, doctor. We have given up those barbarous medicines.'

" 'Whatna kind o' medicines hae ye noo in the Sooth?'

" 'Well, you see, Doctor MacLure, we're homeopathists, and I've my little chest here,' and oot Hopps comes wi' his boxy.

" 'Let's see't,' an' MacLure sits doon and taks oot the bit bottles, and he reads the names wi' a lauch every time.

" 'Belladonna; did ye ever hear the like? Aconite; it cowes a'. Nux Vomica. What next? Weel, ma mannie,' he says tae Hopps, 'it's a fine ploy, and ye 'ill better gang on wi' the Nux till it's dune, and gie him ony ither o' the sweeties he fancies.

" 'Noo, Hillocks, a' maun be aff tae see Drumsheugh's grieve, for he's doon wi' the fever, and it's tae be a teuch fecht. A' henna time tae wait for dinner; gie me some cheese an' cake in ma haund, and Jess 'ill tak a pail o' meal an' water.

" 'Fee; a'm no wantin' yir fees, man; wi' that boxy ye dinna need a doctor; na, na, gie yir siller tae some puir body, Maister Hopps,' an' he was doon the road as hard as he cud lick."

His fees were pretty much what the folk chose to give him, and he collected them once a year at Kildrummie fair.

"Weel, doctor, what am a' awin' ye for the wife and bairn? Ye 'ill need three notes that nicht ye stayed in the hoose an' a' the veesits."

"Havers," MacLure would answer, "prices are low, a'm hearing; gie's thirty shillings."

"No, a'll no, or the wife 'ill take ma ears off," and it was settled for two pounds.

Lord Kilspindie gave him a free house and fields, and one way or other, Drumsheugh told me, the doctor might get in about 150 a year, out of which he had to pay his old housekeeper's wages and a boy's, and keep two horses, besides the cost of instruments and books, which he bought through a friend in Edinburgh with much judgment.

There was only one man who ever complained of the doctor's charges, and that was the new farmer of Milton, who was so good that he was above both churches, and held a meeting in his barn. (It was Milton the Glen supposed at first to be a Mormon, but I can't go into that now.) He offered MacLure a pound less than he asked, and two tracts, whereupon MacLure expressed his opinion of Milton, both from a theological and social standpoint, with such vigour and frankness that an attentive audience of Drumtochty men could hardly contain themselves.

Jamie Soutar was selling his pig at the time, and missed the meeting, but he hastened to condole with Milton, who was complaining everywhere of the doctor's language.

"Ye did richt tae resist him; it 'ill maybe roose the Glen tae mak a stand; he fair hauds them in bondage.

"Thirty shillings for twal veesits, and him no mair than seven mile awa, an' a'm telt there werena mair than four at nicht.

"Ye 'ill hae the sympathy o' the Glen, for a'body kens yir as free wi' yir siller as yir tracts.

"Wes't 'Beware o' gude warks' ye offered him? Man, ye chose it weel, for he's been colleckin' sae mony thae forty years, a'm feared for him.

"A've often thocht oor doctor's little better than the Gude Samaritan, an' the Pharisees didna think muckle o' his chance aither in this warld or that which is tae come."

II

THROUGH THE FLOOD

DOCTOR MACLURE DID NOT LEAD A SOLEMN PROCESSION from the sick bed to the dining-room, and give his opinion from the hearthrug with an air of wisdom bordering on the supernatural, because neither the Drumtochty houses nor his manners were on that large scale. He was accustomed to deliver himself in the yard, and to conclude his directions with one foot in the stirrup; but when he left the room where the life of Annie Mitchell was ebbing slowly away, our doctor said not one word, and at the sight of his face her husband's heart was troubled.

He was a dull man, Tammas, who could not read the meaning of a sign, and laboured under a perpetual disability of speech; but love was eyes to him that day, and a mouth.

"Is't as bad as yir lookin', doctor? Tell's the truth; wull Annie no come through?" and Tammas looked MacLure straight in the face, who never flinched his duty or said smooth things.

"A' wud gie onything tae say Annie hes a chance, but a' daurna; a' doot yir gaein' tae lose her, Tammas."

MacLure was in the saddle, and as he gave his judgment, he laid his hand on Tammas's shoulder with one of the rare caresses that pass between men.

"It's a sair business, but ye 'ill play the man and no vex Annie; she 'ill dae her best, a'll warrant."

"An' a'll dae mine," and Tammas gave MacLure's hand a grip that would have crushed the bones of a weakling. Drumtochty felt in such moments the brotherliness of this rough-looking man, and loved him.

Tammas hid his face in Jess's mane, who looked round with sorrow in her beautiful eyes, for she had seen many tragedies, and in this silent sympathy the stricken man drank his cup, drop by drop.

"A' wesna prepared for this, for a' aye thocht she wud live the langest. ... She's younger than me by ten years, and never wes ill. ... We've been mairit twal year laist Martinmas, but it's juist like a year the day. ...A' wes never worthy o'her, the bonniest, snoddest (neatest), kindliest lass in the Glen. ...A' never cud mak oot hoo she ever lookit at me, 'at hesna hed ae word tae say aboot her till it's ower late. …She didna cuist up tae me that a' wesna worthy o'her, no her, but aye she said, 'Yir ma ain gudeman, and nane cud be kinder tae me.' …An' a' wes minded tae be kind, but a' see noo mony little trokes a' micht hae dune for her, and noo the time is bye. … Naebody kens hoo patient she wes wi' me, and aye made the best o' mae, an' never pit me tae shame afore the fouk. … An' we never hed ae cross word, no ane in twal year. … We were mair nor man and wife, we were sweethearts a' the time.

…Oh, ma bonnie lass, what 'ill the bairnies an' me dae withoot ye, Annie?"

The winter night was falling fast, the snow lay deep upon the ground, and the merciless north wind moaned through the close as Tammas wrestled with his sorrow dry-eyed, for tears were denied Drumtochty men. Neither the doctor nor Jess moved hand or foot, but their hearts were with their fellow creature, and at length the doctor made a sign to Marget Howe, who had come out in search of Tammas, and now stood by his side.

"Dinna mourn tae the brakin' o' yir hert, Tammas," she said, "as if Annie an' you hed never luved. Neither death nor time can pairt them that luve; there's naethin' in a' the warld sae strong as luve. If Annie gaes frae the sicht o' yir een she 'ill come the nearer tae yir hert. She wants tae see ye, and tae hear ye say that ye 'ill never forget her nicht nor day till ye meet in the land where there's nae pairtin'. Oh, a' ken whata'm sayin', for it's five year noo sin George gied awa, an' he's mair wi' me noo than when he wes in Edinboro' and I wes in Drumtochty."

"Thank ye kindly, Marget; thae are gude words and true, an' ye hev the richt tae say them' but a' canna dae withoot seein' Annie comin' tae meet me in the gloamin', an' gaein' in an' oot the hoose, an' hearing her ca' me by ma name, an' a'll no can tell her that a' luve her when there's nae Annie in the hoose.

"Can naethin' be dune, doctor? Ye savit Flora Cammil, and young Burnbrae, an' yon shepherd's wife Dunleith wy, an' we were a' sae prood o' ye, an' pleased tae think that ye hed keepit deith frae anither hame. Can ye no think o' somethin' tae help Annie, and gie her back tae her man and bairnies?" and Tammas searched the doctor's face in the cold, weird light.

"There's nae pooer in heaven or airth like luve," Marget said to me afterwards; "it maks the weak strong and the dumb tae speak. Oor herts were as water afore Tammas's words, an' a' saw the doctor shake in his saddle. A' never kent till that meenut hoo he hed a share in a'body's grief, an carried the heaviest wecht o' a' the Glen. A' peetied him wi' Tammas lookin' at him sae wistfully, as if he hed the keys o' life and' deith in his hands. But he was honest, and wudna hold oot a false houp tae deceive a sore hert or win escape for himsel'."

"Ye needna plead wi' me, Tamms, to dae the best a' can for yir wife. Man, a' kent her lang afore ye ever luved her; a' brocht her intae the warld, and a' saw her through the fever when she wes a bit lassikee; a' closed her mither's een, and it wes me hed tae tell her she wes an orphan, an' nae man wes better pleased when she got a gude husband and a' helpit wi' her fower bairns. A've neither wife nor bairns o' ma own, an' a' coont a' the fouk o' the Glen ma family. Div ye think a' wudna save Annie if I cud? If there wes a man in Muirtown 'at cud dae mir for her, a'd have him this verra nicht, but a' the doctors in Perthshire are helpless for this tribble.

"Tammas, ma puir fallow, if it could avail, a' tell ye a' wud lay doon this auld worn-oot ruckle o' a body o' mine juist tae see ye baith sittin' at the fireside, an' the bairns roond ye, couthy an' canty again; but it's no tae be, Tammas, it's no tae be."

"When a' lookit at the doctor's face," Marget said, "a' thocht him the winsomest man a' ever saw. He wes transfigured that nicht, for a'm judging there's nae transfiguration like luve."

"It's God's will an' maun be borne, but it's a sair wull for me, an' a'm no ungratefu' tae you, doctor, for a' ye've dune and what ye said the nicht," and Tammas went back to sit with Annie for the last time.

Jess picked her way through the deep snow to the main road, with a skill that came of long experience, and the doctor held converse with her according to his wont.

"Eh, Jess wumman, yon wes the hardest wark a' hae tae face, and a' wud rather hae ta'en ma chance o' anither row in a Glen Urtach drift than tell Tammas Mitchell his wife wes deein'.

"A' said she cudna be cured, and it wes true, for there's juist ae man in the land fit for't, and they micht as weel try tae get the mune oot o' heaven. Sae a' said naethin' tae vex Tammas's hert, for it's heavy eneuch withoot regrets.

"But it's hard, Jess, that money wull buy life after a', an' if Annie wes a duchess her man wudna lose her; but nein' only a puir cottar's wife, she maun dee afore the week's oot.

"Gin we hed him the morn there's little doot she wud be saved, for he hesna lost mair than five per cent o' his cases, and they ill be puir toon's craturs, no strappin' women like Annie.

"It's oot o' the question, Jess, say hurry up, lass, for we've hed a heavy day. But it wud be the grandest thing that was ever dune in the Glen in oor time if it could be managed by hook or crook.

"We 'ill gang and see Drumsheugh, Jess; he's anither man sin' Geordie Hoo's deith, and he wes aye kinder than fouk kent"; and the doctor passed at a gallop through the village, whose lights shone across the white frost-bound road.

"Come in by, doctor; a' heard ye on the road; ye 'ill hae been at Tammas Mitchell's; hoo's the gudewife" a' doot she's sober."

"Annie's deein', Drumsheugh, an' Tammas is like tae brak his hert."

"That's no lichtsome, doctor, no lichtsome ava, for a' dinna ken ony man in Drumtochty sae bund up in his wife as Tammas, and there's no a bonnier wumman o' her age crosses our kirk door than Annie, nor a cleverer at her wark. Man, ye 'ill need tae pit yir brains in steep. Is she clean beyond ye?"

"Beyond me and every ither in the land but ane, and it wud cost a hundred guineas tae bring him tae Drumtochty."

"Certes, he's no blate; it's a fell charge for a short day's work; but hundred or no hundred we 'ill hae him, an' no let Annie gang, and her no half her years."

"Are ye meaning it, Drumsheugh?" and MacLure turned white below the tan.

"William MacLure," said Drumsheugh, in one of the few confidences that ever broke the Drumtochty reserve, "a'm a lonely man, wi' naebody o' ma ain blude tae care for me livin', or tae lift me intae ma coffin when a'm deid.

"A' fecht awa a Muirtown market for an extra pund on a beast, or a shillin' on the quarter o' barley, an' what's the gude o't? Burnbrae gaes aff tae get a goon for his wife or a buke for his college laddie, an' Lachlan Campbell 'ill no leave the place noo withoot a ribbon for Flora.

"Ilka man in the Kildrummie train has some bit fairin' in his pooch for the fouk at hame that he's bocht wi' the siller he won.

"But there's naebody tae be lookin' oot for me, an' comin' doon the road tae meet me, and daffin' (joking) wi' me aboot their fairing, or feeling ma pockets. Ou ay, a've seen it a' at ither hooses, though they tried tae hide it frae me for fear a' wud lauch at them. Me lauch, wi' ma cauld, empty hame!

"Yir the only man kens, Weelum, that I aince luved the noblest wumman in the Glen or onywhere, an' a' luve her still, but wi' anither luve noo.

"She hed given her hert tae anither, or a've thocht a' micht hae won her, though nae man be worthy o' sic a gift. Ma hert turned tae bitterness, but that passed awa beside the brier bush whar George Hoo lay yon said simmer time. Some day a'll tell ye ma story, Weelum, for you an' me are auld friends, and will be till we dee."

MacLure felt beneath the table for Drumsheugh's hand, but neither man looked at the other.

"Weel, a' we can dae noo, Weelum, gin we haena mickle brichtness in oor ain hames, is tae keep the licht frae gaein' oot in anither hoose. Write the telegram, man, and Sandy 'ill send it aff frae Kildrummie this verra nicht, and ye 'ill hae yir man the morn."

"Yir the man a' counted ye, Drumsheugh, but ye 'ill grant me ae favour. Ye 'ill let me pay the half, bit by bit—a' ken yir wullin' tae dae't a',—but a' haena mony pleasures, an' a' wud like tae hae ma ain share in savin' Annie's life."

Next morning a figure received Sir George on the Kildrummie platform, whom that famous surgeon took for a gillie, but who introduced himself as "MacLure of Drumtochty." It seemed as if the East had come to meet the West when these two stood together, the one in traveling furs, handsome and distinguished, with his strong, cultured face and carriage of authority, a characteristic type of his profession; and the other more marvelously dressed than ever, for Drumsheugh's topcoat had been forced upon him for the occasion, his face and neck one redness with the bitter cold; rough and ungainly, yet not without some signs of power in his eye and voice, the most heroic type of his noble profession. MacLure compassed the precious arrival with observances till he was securely seated in Drumsheugh's dogcart—a vehicle that lent itself to history—with two full-sized plaids added to his equipment—Drumsheugh and Hillocks had both been requisitioned—and MacLure wrapped another plaid round a leather case, which was placed below the seat with such reverence as might be given to the Queen's regalia. Peter attended their departure full of interest, and as soon as they were in the fir woods MacLure explained that it would be an eventful journey.

"It's a' richt in here, for the wind disna get at the snaw, but the drifts are deep in the Glen, and th' 'ill be some engineerin' afore we get tae oor destination."

Four times they left the road and took their way over fields, twice they forced a passage through a slap in a dyke, thrice they used gaps in the paling which MacLure had made on his downward journey.

"A' seleckit the road this mornin', an' a' ken the depth tae an inch; we 'ill get through this steadin' here tae the main road, but oor worst job 'ill be crossin' the Tochty.

"Ye see the bridge hes been shakin' wi' this winter's flood, and we daurna venture on it, sae we hev tae ford, and the snaw's been melting up Urtach way. There's nae doot the water's gey big, and it's threatenin' tae tise, but we 'ill win through wi' a warstle.

"It micht be safer tae lift the instruments oot o' reach o' the water; wud ye mind haddin' them on yir knee till we're ower, an' keep firm in yir seat in case we come on a stane in the bed o' the river?"

By this time they had come to the edge, and it was not a cheering sight. The Tochty had spread out over the meadows, and while they waited they could see it cover another two inches on the trunk of a tree. There are summer floods, when the water is brown and flecked with foam, but this was a winter flood, which is black and sullen, and runs in the centre with a strong, fierce, silent current. Upon the opposite side Hillocks stood to give directions by word and hand, as the ford was on his land, and none knew the Tochty better in all its ways.

They passed through the shallow water without mishap, save when the wheel struck a hidden stone or fell suddenly into a rut; but when they neared the body of the river MacLure halted, to give Jess a minute's breathing.

"It 'ill tak ye a' yir time, lass, an' a' wud rather be on yir back; but ye never failed me yet, and a wumman's life is hangin' on the crossin'."

With the first plunge into the bed of the stream the water rose to the axles, and then it crept up to the shafts, so that the surgeon could feel it lapping in about his feet, while the dogcart began to quiver, and it seemed as if it were to be carried away. Sir George was as brave as most men, but he had never forded a Highland river in flood, and the mass of black water racing past beneath, before, behind him, affected his imagination and shook his nerves. He rose from his seat and ordered MacLure to turn back, declaring that he would be condemned utterly and eternally if he allowed himself to be drowned for any person.

"Sit doon," thundered MacLure; "condemned ye will be suner or later gin ye shirk yir duty, but through the water ye gang the day."

Both men spoke much more strongly and shortly, but this is what they intended to say, and it was MacLure that prevailed.

Jess trailed her feet along the ground with cunning art, and held her shoulder against the stream; MacLure leant forward in his seat, a rein in each hand, and his eyes fixed on Hillocks, who was now standing up to the waist in the water, shouting directions and cheering on horse and driver.

"Haud tae the richt, doctor; there's a hole yonder. Keep oot o't for ony sake. That's it; yir daein' fine. Steady, man, steady. Yir at the deepest; sit heavy in yir seats. Up the channel noo, and ye'll be oot o' the swirl. Weel dune, Jess, weel dune, auld mare! Mak straicht for me, doctor, an' a'll gie ye the road oot. Ma word, ye've dune yir best, baith o' ye this mornin'," cried Hillocks, splashing up to the dogcart, now in the shallows.

"Sall, it wes titch an' go for a meenut in the middle; a Hielan' ford is a kittle (hazardous) road in the snaw time, but ye're safe noo.

"Gude luck tae ye up at Westerton, sir; nane but a richt-hearted man wud hae riskit the Tochty in flood. Ye're boond tae succeed aifter sic a graund beginnin'," for it had spread already that a famous surgeon had come to do his best for Annie, Tammas Mitchell's wife.

Two hours later MacLure came out from Annie's room and laid hold of Tammas, a heap of speechless misery by the kitchen fire, and carried him off to the barn, and spread some corn on the threshing floor and thrust a flail into his hands.

"Noo we've tae begin, an' we 'ill no be dune for an hoor, and ye've tae lay on withoot stoppin' till a' come for ye, an' a'll shut the door tae haud in the noise, an' keep yir dog beside ye, for there maunna be a cheep aboot the hoose for Annie's sake."

"A'll dae onything ye want me, but if—if———"

"A'll come for ye, Tammas, gin there be danger; but what are ye feared for wi' the Queen's ain surgeon here?"

Fifty minutes did the flail rise and fall, save twice, when Tammas crept to the door and listened, the dog lifting his head and whining.

It seemed twelve hours instead of one when the door swung back, and MacLure filled the doorway, preceded by a great burst of light, for the sun had arisen on the snow.

His face was as tidings of great joy, and Elspeth told me that there was nothing like it to be seen that afternoon for glory, save the sun itself in the heavens.

"A never saw the marrow o't, Tammas, an' a'll never see the like again; it's a' ower, man, withoot a hitch frae beginnin' tae end, and she's fa'in asleep as fine as ye like."

"Dis he think Annie ...'ill live?"

"Of coorse he dis, and be aboot the hoose inside a month; that's the gude a' bein a clean-bluided, weel-livin'———"

"Preserve ye, man, what's wrang wi' ye? It's a mercy a' keppit ye, or we wud hev hed anither job for Sir George.

"Ye're a' richt noo; sit doon on the strae. A'll come back in a whilie, an' ye''ill see Annie juist for a meenut, but ye maunna say a word."

Marget took him in and let him kneel by Annie's bedside.

He said nothing then or afterwards, for speech came only once in his lifetime to Tammas, but Annie whispered, "Ma ain dear man."

When the doctor placed the precious bag beside Sir George in our solitary first next morning, he laid a cheque beside it and was about to leave.

"No, no," said the great man. "Mrs. MacFadyen and I were on the gossip last night, and I know the whole story about you and your friend.

"You have some right to call me a coward, but I'll never let you count me a mean, miserly rascal," and the cheque with Drumsheugh's painful writing fell in fifty pieces on the floor.

As the train began to move, a voice from the first called so that all in the station heard.

"Give's another shake of your hand, MacLure; I'm proud to have met you; you are an honour to our profession. Mind the antiseptic dressings."

It was market day, but only Jamie Soutar and Hillocks had ventured down.

"Did ye hear yon, Hillocks? Hoo dae ye feel? A'll no deny a'm lifted."

Halfway to the Junction Hillocks had recovered, and began to grasp the situation.

"Tell's what he said. A' wud like to hae it exact for Drumsheugh."

"Thae's the eedentical words, an' they're true; there's no man in Drumtochty disna ken that, except ane."

"An' wha's that, Jamie?"

"It's Weelum MacLure himself. Man, a've often girned that he sud fecht awa for us a', and maybe dee before he kent that he hed gathered mair luve than ony man in the Glen.

" 'A'm prood tae hae met ye,' says Sir George, an' him the greatest doctor in the land. 'Yir an honor tae oor-profession.'

"Hillocks, a' wudna hae missed it for twenty notes," said James Soutar, cynic-in-ordinary to the parish of Drumtochty.

III

A FIGHT WITH DEATH

WHEN DRUMSHEUGH'S GRIEVE WAS BROUGHT TO THE gates of death by fever, caught, as was supposed, on an adventurous visit to Glasgow, the London doctor at Lord Kilspindie's shooting lodge looked in on his way from the moor, and declared it impossible for Saunders to live through the night.

"I give him six hours, more or less; it is only a question of time," said the oracle, buttoning his gloves and getting into the brake; "tell your parish doctor that I was sorry not to have met him."

Bell heard this verdict from behind the door, and gave way utterly, but Drumsheugh declined to accept it as final, and devoted himself to consolation.

"Dinna greet like that, Bell wumman, sae lang as Saunders is still livin'; a'll never give up houp, for ma pairt, till oor ain man says the word.

"A' the doctors in the land dinna ken as muckle aboot us as Weelum MacLure, an' he's ill tae beat when he's trying tae save a man's life."

MacLure, on his coming, would say nothing, either weal or woe till he had examined Saunders. Suddenly his face turned into iron before their eyes, and he looked like one encountering a merciless foe. For there was a feud between MacLure and a certain mighty power which had lasted for forty years in Drumtochty.

"The London doctor said that Saunders wud sough awa afore mornin', did he? Weel, he's an authority on fevers an' sic like diseases, an' ought tae ken.

"It's may be presumptuous o' me tae differ frae him, and it wudna be verra respectfu' o' Saunders tae live aifter this opeenion. But Saunders wes aye thraun an' ill tae drive, an' he's as like as no tae gang his ain gait.

"A'm no meanin' tae reflect on sae clever a man. But he didna ken the seetuation. He can read fevers like a buik, but he never cam across sic a thing as the Drumtochty constitution a' his days.

"Ye see, when onybody gets a low as puir Saunders, here, it's juist a hand to hand wrestle atween the fever and his constitution, an' of coorse, if he hed been a shilpit, stuntit, feckless effeegy o' a cratur, fed on tea an' made dishes and pushioned wi' bad air, Saunders wud hae nae chance; he wes boond tae gae oot like the snuff o' a candle.

"But Saunders hes been fillin' his lungs for five and thirty year wi' strong Drumtochty air, an' eatin' naethin' but kirny aitmeal, and drinkin' naethin' but fresh milk frae the coo, an' followin' the ploo through the new-turned, sweet-smelling earth, an' swingin' the scythe in haytime and harvest, till the legs an' airms o' him were iron, an' his chest wes like the cuttin' o' an oak tree.

"He's a waesome sicht the nicht, but Saunders wes a buirdly man aince, and wull never lat his life be taken lichtly frae him. Na, Na, he hesna sinned against Nature, and Nature 'ill stand by him noo in his oor o' distress.

"A' daurna say yea, Bell, muckle as a' wud like, for this is an evil disease, cunnin' an' treacherous as the devil himself, but a' winna say nay, sae keep yir hert frae despair.

"It wull be a sair fecht, but it 'ill be settled one wy or anither by sax o'clock the morn's morn. Nae man can prophecee hoo it 'ill end, but ae thing is certain, a'll no see deith tak a Drumtochty man afore his time if a' can help it.

"Noo, Bell ma wumman, yir near deid wi' tire, an' nae wonder. Ye've dune a' ye cud for yir man, an' ye 'ill lippen (trust) him the nicht tae Drumsheugh an' me; we 'ill no fail him or you.

"Lie doon an' rest, an' if it be the wull o' the Almichty a'll wauken ye in the mornin' tae see a livin' conscious man, an' if it be itherwise a'll come for ye the suner, Bell," and the big red hand went out to the anxious wife. "A' gie ye ma word."

Bell leant over the bed, and at the sight of Saunders' face a superstitious dread seized her.

"See, doctor, the shadow of deith is on him that never lifts. A've seen it afore, on ma father an' mither. A' canna leave him, a' canna leave him."

"It's hoverin', Bell, but it hesna fallen; please God it never wull. Gang but and get some sleep, for it's time we were at oor work.

"The doctors in the toons hae nurses an' a' kinds o' handy apparatus," said MacLure to Drumsheugh when Bell had gone, "but you an' me 'ill need tae be nurse the nicht, an' use sic things as we hev.

"It 'ill be a lang nicht and anxious wark, but a wud rather hae ye, auld freend, wi' me than ony man in the Glen. Ye're no feared tae gie a hand?"

"Me feared? No likely. Man, Saunders cam tae me a haflin, and hes been on Drumsheugh for twenty years, an' though he be a dour chiel, he's a faithfu' servant as ever lived. It's awesome tae see him lyin' there moanin' like some dumb animal frae mornin' tae night, an' no able tae answer his ain wife when she speaks.

"Div ye think, Weelum, he hes a chance?"

"That he hes, at ony rate, and it 'ill no be your blame or mine if he hesna mair."

While he was speaking, MacLure took off his coat and waistcoat and hung them on the back of the door. Then he rolled up the sleeves of his shirt and laid bare two arms that were nothing but bone and muscle.

"It gar'd ma very blood rin faster tae the end of ma fingers juist tae look at him," Drumsheugh expatiated afterwards to Hillocks, "for a' saw noo that there was tae be a stand-up fecht atween him an' deith for Saunders, and when a' thocht o' Bell an' her bairns, a' kent wha wud win.

" 'Aff wi' yir coat, Drumsheugh,' said MacLure; 'ye 'ill need tae bend yir back the nicht' gather a' the pails in the hoose and fill them at the spring, an' a'll come doon tae help ye wi' the carryin'.' "

It was a wonderful ascent up the steep pathway from the spring to the cottage on its little knoll, the two men in single file, bareheaded, silent, solemn, each with a pail of water in either hand, MacLure limping painfully in front, Drumsheugh blowing behind; and when they laid down their burden in the sick room, where the bits of furniture had been put to a side and a large tub held the centre, Drumsheugh looked curiously at the doctor.

"No, a'm no daft; ye needna be feared' but yir tae get yir first lesson in medicine the nicht, an' if we win the battle ye can set up for yersel in the Glen.

"There's twa dangers—that Saunders' strength fails, an' that the force o' the fever grows; and we have juist two weapons.

"Yon milk on the drawers' head an' the bottle of whisky is tae keep up the strength, and this cool caller water is tae keep doon the fever.

"We 'ill cast oot the fever by the virtue o' the earth an' the water."

"Div ye mean tae pit Saunders in the tub?"

"Ye hiv it noo, Drumsheugh, and that's hoo a' need yir help."

"Man, Hillocks," Drumsheugh used to moralize, as often as he

47

remembered that critical night, "it wes humblin' tae see hoo low sickness can bring a pooerfu' man an' ocht tae keep us frae pride.

"A month syne there wesna a stronger man in the Glen than Saunders, an' noo he wes juist a bundle o' skin and bone, that neither saw nor heard, nor moved nor felt, that kent naethin' that was dune tae him.

"Hillocks, a' wudna hae wished ony man tae hev seen Saunders—for it wull never pass frae before ma een as long as a' live—but a' wish a' the Glen hed stude by MacLure kneelin' on the floor wi' his sleeves up tae his oxters and waitin' on Saunders.

"Yon big man wes as pitifu' an' gentle as a wumman, and when he laid the puir fallow in his bed again, he happit him ower as a mither dis her bairn."

Thrice it was done, Drumsheugh ever bringing up colder water from the spring, and twice MacLure was silent, but after the third time there was a gleam in his eye.

"We're haudin' oor ain; we're no bein' maistered, at ony rate; mair a' canna say for three oors.

"We 'ill no need the water again, Drumsheugh; gae oot and tak a breath o' air; a'm on gaird masel."

It was an hour before daybreak, and Drumsheugh wandered through fields he had trodden since childhood. The cattle lay sleeping in the pastures; their shadowy forms, with a patch of whiteness here and there, having a weird suggestion of death. He heard the burn running over the stones; fifty years ago he had made a dam that lasted till winter. The hooting of an owl made him start; one had frightened him as a boy so that he ran home to his mother—she died thirty years ago. The smell of ripe corn filled the air; it would soon be cut and garnered. He could see the dim outlines of his house, all dark and cold; no one he loved was beneath the roof. The lighted window in Saunders' cottage told where a man hung between life and death, but love was in that home. The futility of life arose before this lonely man, and overcame his heart with an indescribable sadness. What a vanity was all human labour, what a mystery all human life.

But while he stood, a subtle change came over the night, and the air trembled round him as if one had whispered. Drumsheugh lifted his head and looked eastwards. A faint grey stole over the distant horizon, and suddenly a cloud reddened before his eyes. The sun was not in sight, but was rising, and sending forerunners before his face. The cattle began to stir, a blackbird burst into song, and before Drumsheugh crossed the threshold of Saunders' house, the first ray of the sun had broken on a peak of the Grampians.

MacLure left the bedside, and as the light of the candle fell on the doctor's face, Drumsheugh could see that it was going well with Saunders.

"He's nae waur; an' it's half six noo; it's ower sune tae say mair, but a'm houpin' for the best. Sit doon and take a sleep, for ye're needin' 't, Drumsheugh,, an', man, ye hae worked for it."

As he dozed off, the last thing Drumsheugh saw was the doctor sitting erect in his chair, a clenched fist resting on the bed, and his eyes already bright with the vision of victory.

He awoke with a start to find the room flooded with the morning sunshine, and every trace of last night's work removed.

The doctor was bending over the bed, and speaking to Saunders.

"It's me, Saunders, Doctor MacLure, ye ken; dinna try tae speak or move; juist let this drap o milk slip ower-ye 'ill be needin' yir breakfast, lad—and gang tae sleep again."

Five minutes, and Saunders had fallen into a deep, healthy sleep, all tossing and moaning come to an end. Then MacLure stepped softly across the floor, picked up his coat and waistcoat, and went out at the door.

Drumsheugh arose and followed him without a word. They passed through the little garden, sparkling with dew, and beside the byre, where Hawkie rattled her chain, impatient for Bell's coming, and by Saunders' little strip of corn ready for the scythe, till they reached an open field. There they came to a halt, and Doctor MacLure for once allowed himself to go.

His coat he flung east and his waistcoat west, as far as he could hurl them, and it was plain he would have shouted had he been a complete mile from Saunders' room. Any less distance was useless for adequate expression. He struck Drumsheugh a mighty blow that well-nigh leveled that substantial man in the dust, and then the doctor of Drumtochty issued his bulletin.

"Saunders wesna tae live through the nicht, but he's livin' this meenut, an' like to live.

"He's got by the warst clean and fair, and wi' him that's as good as cure.

"It 'ill be a graund waukenin' for Bell; she 'ill no be a weedow yet, nor the bairnies fatherless.

"There's nae use glowerin' at me, Drumsheugh, for a body's daft at a time, an' a' canna contain masel, and a'm no gaein' tae try."

Then it dawned upon Drumsheugh that the doctor was attempting the Highland fling.

"He's ill made tae begin wi'," Drumsheugh explained in the kirkyard next Sabbath, "and ye ken he's been terrible mishannelled by accidents, sae ye may think what like it wes, but, as sure as deith, o' a' the Hielan flings a' ever saw yon wes the bonniest.

"A' hevna shaken ma ain legs for thirty years, but a' confess tae a turn masel. Ye may lauch an' ye like, neeburs, but the thocht o' Bell and' the news that wes waitin' her got the better o' me.

Drumtochty did not laugh. Drumtochty looked as if it could have done quite otherwise for joy.

"A' wud hae made a third gin a' hed been there," announced Hillocks, aggressively.

"Come on, Drumsheugh," said Jamie Soutar, "gie's the end o't; it wes a michty mornin'."

" 'We're twa auld fules,' says MacLure tae me, and he gaithers up his claithes. 'It wud set us better tae be tellin' Bell.'

"She wes sleepin' on top o' her bed wrapped in a plaid, fair worn oot wi' three weeks' nursing o' Saunders, but at the first touch she was oot upon the floor.

" 'Is Saunders deein', doctor?' she cries. 'Ye promised tae wauken me; dinna tell me it's a' ower.'

" 'There's nae deein' aboot him, Bell; ye're no tae lose yir man this time, sae far as a' can see. Come ben and' jidge for yersel'.'

"Bell lookit at Saunders, and the tears of joy fell on the bed like rain.

" 'The shadow's lifted,' she said; 'he's come back frae the mooth o' the tomb.

" 'A' prayed last nicht that the Lord wud leave Saunders till the laddies cud dae for themselves, an' thae words came intae ma mind, "Weepin' may endure for a nicht, but joy cometh in the mornin'."

" 'The Lord heard ma prayer, and joy hes come in the mornin',' an' she gripped the doctor's hand.

" 'Ye've been the instrument, Doctor MacLure. Ye wudna gie him up, and ye did what nae ither cud for him, an' a've ma man the day, and the bairns hae their father.'

"An' afore MacLure kent what she was daein', Bell lifted his hand to her lips and kissed it."

"Did she, though?" cried Jamie. "Wha wud hae thocht there wes as muckle spunk in Bell?"

"MacLure, of coorse, was clean scandalized," continued Drumsheugh, "an' pooed awa his hand as if it hed been burned.

"Nae man can thole that kind o' fraikin', and a' never heard o' sic a thing in the parish, but we maun excuse Bell, neeburs; it wes an occasion by ordinar," and Drumsheugh made Bell's apology to Drumtochty for such an excess of feeling.

"A' see naethin' tae excuse," insisted Jamie, who was in great fettle that Sabbath; "the doctor hes never been burdened wi' fees, and a'm judgin' he counted a wumman's gratitude that he saved frae weedowhood the best he ever got."

"A' gaed up tae the Manse last nicht," concluded Drumsheugh, "and telt the minister hoo the doctor focht oors for Saunders' life, an' won, and ye never saw a man sae carried. He walkit up and doon the room a' the time, and every other meenut he blew his nose like a trumpet.

" 'I've got a cold in my head tonight, Drumsheugh,' says he; 'never mind me.' "

"A've hed the same masel in sic circumstances; they come on sudden," said Jamie.

"A' wager there 'ill be a new bit in the laist prayer the day, an' somethin' worth hearin'."

And the fathers went into kirk in great expectation.

"We beseech Thee for such as be sick, that Thy hand may be on them for good, and that Thou wouldst restore them again to health and strength," was the familiar petition of every Sabbath.

The congregation waited in a silence that might be heard, and were not disappointed that morning, for the minister continued:

"Especially we tender Thee hearty thanks that Thou didst spare thy servant who was brought down into the dust of death, and hast given him back to his wife and children, and unto that end didst wonderfully bless the skill of him who goes out and in amongst us, the beloved physician of this parish and adjacent districts."

"Didna a' tell ye, neeburs?" said Jamie, as they stood at the kirkyard gate before dispersing; "there's no a man in the county cud hae dune it better. 'Beloved physician,' an' his 'skill,' tae, an' bringing in 'adjacent districts'; that's Glen Urtach; it wes handsome, and the doctor earned it, ay, every word.

"It's an awfu' peety he didna hear yon; but dear knows whar he is the day, maist likely up——"

Jamie stopped suddenly at the sound of a horse's feet, and there, coming down the avenue of beech trees that made a long vista from the kirk gate, they saw the doctor and Jess.

One thought flashed through the minds of the fathers of the commonwealth.

It ought to be done as he passed, and it would be done if it were not Sabbath. Of course it was out of the question on Sabbath.

The doctor is now distinctly visible, riding after his fashion.

There was never such a chance, if it were only Saturday; and each man reads his own regret in his neighbor's face.

The doctor is nearing them rapidly; they can imagine the shepherd's tartan.

Sabbath or no Sabbath, the Glen cannot let him pass without some tribute of their pride.

Jess has recognized friends, and the doctor is drawing rein.

"It hes tae be dune," said Jamie desperately, "say what ye like." Then they all looked towards him, and Jamie led.

"Hurrah," swinging his Sabbath hat in the air, "hurrah," and once more, "hurrah," Whinnie Knowe, Drumsheugh, and Hillocks joining lustily, but Tammas Mitchell carrying all before him, for he had found at last an expression for his feelings that rendered speech unnecessary.

It was a solitary experience for horse and rider, and Jess bolted without delay. But the sound followed and surrounded them, and as they passed the corner of the kirkyard, a figure waved his college cap over the wall and gave a cheer on his own account.

"God Bless you, doctor, and well done."

"If it isna the minister," cried Drumsheugh, "in his goon an bans; tae think o' that; but a' respeck him for it."

Then Drumtochty became self-conscious, and went home in confusion of face and unbroken silence, except Jamie Soutar, who faced his neighbors at the parting of the ways without shame.

"A wud dae it a' ower again if a' hed the chance; he got naethin' but his due."

It was two miles before Jess composed her mind, and the doctor and she could discuss it quietly together.

"A' can hardly believe ma ears, Jess, an' the Sabbath tae; their verra jidgdment hes gane frae the fouk o' Drumtochty.

"They've heard about Saunders, a'm thinkin', wumman, and they're pleased we brocht him roond; he's fairly on the mend, ye ken, noo.

"A' never expeckit the like o' this, though, and it wes juist a wee thingie mair than a' cud hae stude.

"Ye hev yir share in't tae, lass; we've hed mony a hard nicht and day thegither, an' yon wes oor reward. No mony men in this warld 'ill ever get a better, for it cam frae the hert o' honest fouk."

IV

THE DOCTOR'S LAST JOURNEY

DRUMTOCHTY HAD A VIVID RECOLLECTION OF THE winter when Dr. MacLure was laid up for two months with a broken leg, and the Glen was dependent on the dubious ministrations of the Kildrummie doctor. Mrs. MacFadyen also pretended to recall a "whup" of some kind or other he had in the fifties, but this was considered to be rather a pyrotechnic display of Elspeth's superior memory than a serious statement of fact. MacLure could not have ridden through the snow of forty winters without suffering, yet no one ever heard him complain, and he never pled illness to any messenger by night or day.

"It took me," said Jamie Soutar to Milton afterwards, "the feck o' ten meenuts tae howk him an' Jess oot ae snawy nicht when Drums turned bad sudden, and if he didna try to excuse himself for no hearing me at aince wi' some story aboot juist comin' in frae Glen Urtach, and no bein' in his bed for the laist twa nichts.

"He wes that carefu' o' himself an' lazy that if it hedna been for the siller, a've often thocht, Milton, he wud never hae dune a handstroke o' wark in the Glen.

"What scunnered me wes the wy the bairns were ta'en in wi' him. Man, a've seen him tak a wee laddie on his knee that his ain mither cudna quiet, an' lilt 'Sing a song o' saxpence' till the bit mannie wud be lauchin' like a gude ane, an' pooin' the doctor's beard.

"As for the weemen, he fair cuist a glamour ower them; they're daein' naethin' noo but speak aboot this body and the ither he cured, an' hoo he aye hed a couthy word for sick fouk. Weemen hae nae discernment, Milton; tae hear them speak ye wud think MacLure hed been a releegious man like yersel, although, as ye said, he wes little mair than a Gallio.

"Bell Baxter was haverin' awa in the shop tae sic an extent aboot the wy MacLure brocht roond Saunders when he hed the fever that a' gied oot at the door, a' wes that disgusted, an' a'm telt when Tammas Mitchell heard the news in the smiddy he wes juist on the greeting.

"The smith said that he wes thinkin' o' Annie's tribble, but ony wy a' ca' it rael bairnly. It's no like Drumtochty; ye're setting an example, Milton,

54

wi' yir composure. But a' mind ye took the doctor's measure as sune as ye cam intae the pairish."

It is the penalty of a cynic that he must have some relief for his secret grief, and Milton began to weary of life in Jamie's hands during those days.

Drumtochty was not observant in the matter of health, but they had grown sensitive about Dr. MacLure, and remarked in the kirkyard all summer that he was failing.

"He wes aye spare," said Hillocks, "an' he's beeb sair twisted for the laist twenty year, but a' never mind him booed till the year. An' he's gaein' intae sma' buke (bulk), an' a' dinna like that, neeburs.

"The Glen wudna dae weel withoot Weelum MacLure, an' he's no as young as he wes. Man, Drumsheugh, ye micht wile him aff tae the saut water atween the neeps and the hairst. He's been workin' forty year for a holiday, an' it's aboot due."

Drumsheugh was full of tact, and met MacLure quite by accident on the road.

"Saunders 'ill no need me till the shearing begins," he explained to the doctor, "an' a'm gaein' tae Brochty for a turn o' the hot baths; they're fine for the rheumatics.

"Wull ye no come wi' me for auld lang syne? It's lonesome for a solitary man, an' it wud dae ye gude."

"Na, na, Drumsheugh," said MacLure, who understood perfectly, "a've dune a' thae years withoot a break, an' a'm laith (unwilling) tae be takin' holidays at the tail end.

"A'll no be mony months wi' ye a' thegither noo, an' a'm wanting tae spend a' the time a' hev in the Glen. Ye see yersel that a'll sune be getting ma lang rest, an' a'll no deny that a'm wearyin' for it."

As autumn passed into winter, the Glen noticed that the doctor's hair had turned grey, and that his manner had lost all its roughness. A feeling of secret gratitude filled their hearts, and they united in a conspiracy of attention. Annie Mitchell knitted a huge comforter in red and white, which the doctor wore in misery for one whole day, out of respect for Annie, and then hung in his sitting-room as a wall ornament. Hillocks used to intercept him with hot drinks, and one drifting day compelled him to shelter till the storm abated. Flora Campbell brought a wonderful compound of honey and whisky, much tasted in Auchindarroch, for his cough, and the mother of young Burnbrae filled his cupboard with black jam, as a healing measure. Jamie Soutar seemed to have an endless series of jobs in the doctor's direction, and looked in "juist tae rest himself" in the kitchen.

MacLure had been slowly taking in the situation, and at last he unburdened himself one night to Jamie.

"What ails the fouk, think ye? For they're aye lecturin' me noo tae tak care o' the weet and tae wrap masel up, an' there's no a week but they're sendin' bit presents tae the hoose, till a'm fair ashamed."

"Oo, a'll explain that in a meenut," answered Jamie, "for a' ken the Glen weel. Ye see they're juist tryin' the Scripture plan o' heapin' coals o' fire on yer head.

"Here ye've been negleckin' the fouk in seeckness an' lettin' them dee afore their freends' eyes withoot a ficht, an' refusin' tae gang tae a puir wumman in her tribble, an' frichtenin' the bairns—no, a'm no dune—and scourgin' us wi' fees, and livin' yersel on the fat o' the land.

"Ye've been carryin' on this trade ever sin yir father dee'd, and the Glen didna notis. But ma word, they've fund ye oot at laist, an' they're gaein' tae mak ye suffer for a' yir ill usage. Div ye understand noo?" said Jamie, savagely.

For a while MacLure was silent, and then he only said:

"It's little a' did for the puir bodies; but ye hev a gude hert, Jamie, a rael good hert."

It was a bitter December Sabbath, and the fathers were settling the affairs of the parish ankle deep in snow, when MacLure's old housekeeper told Drumsheugh that the doctor was not able to rise, and wished to see him in the afternoon.

"Ay, ay," said Hillocks, shaking his head, and that day Drumsheugh omitted four pews with the ladle, while Jamie was so vicious on the way home that none could endure him.

Janet had lit a fire in the unused grate, and hung a plaid by the window to break the power of the cruel north wind, but the bare room with its half-a-dozen bits of furniture and a worn strip of carpet, and the outlook upon the snow drifted up to the second pane of the window and the black firs laden with their icy burden, sent a chill to Drumsheugh's heart.

The doctor had weakened sadly, and could hardly lift his head, but his face lit up at the sight of his visitor, and the big hand, which was now quite refined in its whiteness, came out from the bed-clothes with the old warm grip.

"Come in by, man, and sit doon; it's an awfu' day tae bring ye sae far, but a' kent ye wudna grudge the traivel.

"A' wesna sure till last nicht, an' then a' felt it wudna be lang, an' a' took a wearyin' this mornin' tae see ye.

"We've been friends sin' we were laddies at the auld schule in the firs, an' a' wud like ye tae be wi' me at the end. Ye 'ill stay the nicht, Paitrick, for auld lang syne."

Drunsheugh was much shaken, and the sound of the Christian name, which he had not heard since his mother's death, gave him a "grue" (shiver), as if one had spoken from the other world.

"It's maist awfu' tae hear ye speakin' aboot deein' Weelum; a' canna bear it. We 'ill hae the Muirtown doctor up, an' ye 'ill be aboot again in nae time.

"Ye hevna ony sair tribble; ye're juist trachled wi' hard wark an' needin' a rest. Dinna say ye're gaein' tae leave us, Weelum; we canna dae withoot ye in Drumtochty;" and Drumsheugh looked wistfully for some word of hope.

"Na, na, Paitrick, naethin' can be dune, an' it's ower late tae send for only doctor. There's a knock that canna be mista'en, an' a' heard it last nicht. A've focht deith for ither fouk mair than forty year, but ma ain time hes come at laist.

"A've nae tribble worth mentionin'—a bit titch o' bronchitis—an' a've hed a graund constitution; but a'm fair worn oot, Paitrick; that's ma complaint, an' it's past curin'."

Drumsheugh went over to the fireplace, and for a while did nothing but break up the smouldering peats, whose smoke powerfully affected his nose and eyes.

"When ye're ready, Paitrick, there's two or three little trokes a' wud like ye tae look aifter, an' a'll tell ye aboot them as lang's ma head's clear.

"A' didna keep buiks, as ye ken, for a' aye hed a guid memory. So naebody 'ill be harried for money aifter ma deith, and ye 'ill hae nae accounts tae collect.

"But the fouk are honest in Drumtochty, and they 'ill be offerin' ye siller, an' a'll gie ye ma mind aboot it. Gin it be a puir body, tell her tae keep it and get a bit plaidie wi' the money, and she 'ill maybe think o' her auld doctor at a time. Gin it be a bien (well-to-do) man, tak half of what he offers, for a Drumtochty man wud scorn to be mean in sic circumstances; and if onybody needs a doctor an' canna pay for him, see he's no left tae dee when a'm oot o' the road."

"Nae fear o' that as lang as a'm livin', Weelum; that hundred's still tae the fore, ye ken, an' a'll tak care it's weel spent.

"Yon wes the best job we ever did thegither, an' dookin' Saunders; ye 'ill no forget that nicht, Weelum"—a gleam came into the doctor's eyes—"tae say naethin' o' the Highlan' fling."

The remembrance of that great victory came upon Drumsheugh, and tried his fortitude.

"What 'ill become o's when ye're no here tae gie a hand in time o' need? We 'ill tak ill wi' a stranger that disna ken ane o's frae anither."

"It's a' for the best, Paitrick, an' ye 'ill see that in a whilie. A've kent fine that ma day wes ower, an' that ye sud hae a younger man.

"A' did what a' cud tae keep up wi' the new medicine, but a' hed little time for readin', and nane for traivellin'.

"A'm the last o' the auld schule, an' a' ken as weel as onybody thet a' wesna sae dainty an' fine-mannered as the town doctors. Ye took me as a' wes, an' naebody ever cuist up tae me that a' wes a plain man. Na, na; ye've been rael kind an' conseederate a' thae years."

"Weelum, gin ye carry on sic nonsense ony langer," interrupted Drumsheugh, huskily, "a'll leave the hoose; a' canna stand it."

"It's the truth, Paitrick, but we 'ill gae on wi' our wark, for a'm failin' fast.

"Gie Janet ony sticks of furniture she needs tae furnish a hoose, and sell a' thing else tae pay the wricht (undertaker) an' bedrel (gravedigger). If the new doctor be a young laddie and no verra rich, ye micht let him hae the buiks an' instruments; it 'ill aye be a help.

"But a' wudna like ye tae sell Jess, for she's been a faithfu' servant, an' a freend tae. There's a note or twa in that drawer a' savit, an' if ye kent ony man that wud gie her a bite o' grass and a sta' in his stable till she followed her maister—"

"Confoond ye, Weelum," broke out Drumsheugh; "it's doonricht cruel o' ye to speak like this tae me. Whar wud Jess gang but tae Drumsheugh?

She 'ill hae her run o' heck an' manger sae lang as she lives; the Glen wudna like tae see anither man on Jess, and nae man 'ill ever touch the auld mare."

"Dinna mind me, Paitrick, for a' expecit this; but ye ken we're no verra gleg wi' oor tongues in Drumtochty. An' dinna tell a' that's in oor herts.

"Weel, that's a' that a' mind, an' the rest a' leave tae yersel. A've neither kith nor kin tae bury me, sae you an' the neeburs 'ill need tae lat me doon; but gin Tammas Mitchel or Saunders be stannin' near and lookin' as if they wud like a cord, gie't tae them, Paitrick. They're both dour chiels, and haena muckle tae say, but Tammas hes a graund hert, and there's waur fouk in the Glen than Saunders.

"A'm getting' drowsy, an' a'll no be able tae follow ye sune, a' doot; wud ye read a bit tae me afore a' fa' ower?

"Ye 'ill find ma mither's Bible on the drawers' heid, but ye 'ill need tae come close tae the bed, for a'm no hearin' or seein' sae weel as a' wes when ye cam."

Drumsheugh put on his spectacles and searched for a comfortable Scripture, while the light of the lamp fell on his shaking hands and the doctor's face, where the shadow was now settling.

"Ma mither aye wantit this read tae her when she wes sober (weak)," and Drumsheugh began, "In my Father's house are many mansions," but MacLure stopped him.

"It's a bonnie word, an' yir mither wes a sanct; but it's no for the like o' me. It's ower gude; a' daurna tak it.

"Shut the buik an' let it open itsel, an' ye 'ill get a bit a've been readin' every nicht the laist month."

Then Drumsheugh found the Parable wherein the Master tells us what God thinks of a Pharisee and of a penitent sinner, till he came to the words: "And the publican, standing afar off, would not lift up so much as his eyes to heaven, but smote upon his breast, saying, God be merciful to me a sinner."

"That micht hae been written for me, Paitrick, or ony ither auld sinner that hes feenished his life, an' hes naethin' tae say for himsel.

"It wasna easy for me tae get tae kirk, but a' cud hae managed wi' a stretch, an' a' used langidge a' sudna, an' a' micht hae been gentler, and no been so short in the temper. A' see't a' noo.

"It's ower late tae mend, but ye 'ill maybe juist say to the fouk that I wes sorry, an' a'm houpin that the Almichty 'ill hae mercy on me.

"Cud ye ...pit up a bit prayer, Paitrick?"

"A' haena the words," said Drumsheugh in great distress; "wud ye like's tae send for the minister?"

"It's no time for that noo, an' a' wud rather hae yersel—juist what's in yir hert, Paitrick: the Almichty 'ill ken the lave (rest) Himsel."

So Drumsheugh knelt and prayed with many pauses.

"Almichty God ... dinna be hard on Weelum MacLure, for he's no been hard wi' onybody in Drumtochty. ... Be kind tae him as he's been tae us a' for forty year. ... We're a' sinners afore Thee. ... Forgive him what he's dune wrang, an' dinna cuist it up tae him. ... Mind the fouk he's helpit ... the weemen an' bairnies ... an' gie him a welcome hame, for he's sair needin't after a' his wark. ... Amen."

"Thank ye, Paitrick, and gude nicht tae ye. Ma ain true freend, gie's yir hand, for a'll may be no ken ye again.

"Noo a'll say ma mither's prayer and hae a sleep, but ye 'ill no leave me till a' is ower."

Then he repeated as he had done every night of his life:

> "This night I lay me down to sleep,
> I pray the Lord my soul to keep.
> And if I die before I wake,
> I pray the Lord my soul to take."

He was sleeping quietly when the wind drove the snow against the window with a sudden "swish"; and he instantly awoke, so to say, in his sleep. Someone needed him.

"Are ye frae Glen Urtach?" and an unheard voice seemed to have answered him.

"Worse is she, an' sufferin' awfu'; that's no lichtsome; ye did richt tae come.

"The front door's drifted up; gang roond tae the back, an' ye 'ill get intae the kitchen: a'll be ready in a meenut.

"Gie's a hand wi' the lantern when a'm saidling Jess, an' ye needna come on till daylicht; a' ken the road."

Then he was away in his sleep on some errand of mercy, and struggling through the storm.

"It's a coorse nicht, Jess, an' heavy traivellin'; can ye see afore ye, lass? For a'm clean confused wi' the snaw; bide a wee till a' find the diveesion o' the roads; it's aboot here back or forrit.

"Steady lass, steady, dinna plunge; it's a drift we're in, but ye're no sinkin';…up noo;…there ye are on the road again.

"Eh, it's deep the nicht, an' hard on us baith, but there's a puir wumman micht dee if we didna warstle through;…that's it; ye ken fine what a'm sayin.

"We 'ill hae tae leave the road here, an' tak tae the muir. Sandie 'ill no can leave the wife alane tae meet us;…feel for yersel', lass, and keep oot o' the holes.

"Yon's the hoose black in the snaw. Sandie! man, ye frichtened us; a' didna see ye ahint the dyke; hoo's the wife?"

After a while he began again:

"Ye're fair dune, Jess, and so a' am masel: we're baith getting' auld, an' dinna tak sae weel wi' the nicht wark.

"We 'ill sune be hame noo; this is the black wood, and it's no lang aifter that; we're ready for oor beds, Jess;…ay, ye like a clap at a time; mony a mile we've gaed thegither.

"Yon's the licht in the kitchen window; nae wonder ye're nickering (neighing);…it's been a stiff journey; a'm tired, lass…a'm tired tae deith," and the voice died into silence.

Drumsheugh held his friend's hand, which now and again tightened in his, and as he watched, a change came over the face on the pillow beside him. The lines of weariness disappeared, as if God's hand had passed over it; and peace began to gather round the closed eyes.

The doctor has forgotten the toil of later years, and has gone back to his boyhood.

"The Lord's my Shepherd, I'll not want,"

he repeated, till he came to the last verse, and then he hesitated.

"Goodness and mercy all my life
Shall surely follow me.

"Follow me...and...and...what's next? Mither said I wes tae haed ready when she cam.

" 'A'll come afore ye gang tae sleep, Wullie, but ye 'ill no get yir kiss unless ye can feenish the psalm.'

"And...in God's house...for evermore my...hoo dis it rin? a' canna mind the next word...my, my—

"It's ower dark noo tae read it, an' mither 'ill sune be comin'."

Drumsheugh, in an agony, whispered into his ear, " 'My dwelling-place,' Weelum."

"That's it, that's it a' noo; wha said it?

> "And in God's house for evermore
> My dwelling-place shall be.

"A'm ready noo, an' a'll get ma kiss when mither comes; a' wish she wud come, for a'm tired an' wantin tae sleep.

"Yon's her step...an' she's carryin' a licht in her hand; a' see it through the door.

"Mither! a' kent ye wudna forget yir laddie, for ye promised tae come, and a've feenished ma psalm.

> "And in God's house for evermore
> My dwelling-place shall be.

"Gie me the kiss, mither, for a've been waitin' for ye, an' a'll sune be asleep."

The grey morning light fell on Drumsheugh, still holding his friends cold hand, and staring at a hearth where the fire had died down into white ashes; but the peace on the doctor's face was of one who rested from his labours.

V

THE MOURNING OF THE GLEN

DR. MACLURE WAS BURIED DURING THE GREAT SNOW-storm, which is still spoken of, and will remain the standard of snowfall in Drumtochty for the century. The snow was deep on the Monday, and the men that gave notice of his funeral had hard work to reach the doctor's distant patients. On Tuesday morning it began to fall again in heavy fleecy flakes, and continued till Thursday, and then on Thursday the north wind rose and swept the snow into the hollows of the roads that went to the upland farms, and built it into a huge bank at the mouth of Glen Urtach, and laid it across our main roads in drifts of every size and the most lovely shapes, and filled up crevices in the hills to the depth of fifty feet.

On Friday morning the wind had sunk to passing gusts that powdered your coat with white, and the sun was shining on one of those winter landscapes no townsman can imagine and no countryman ever forgets. The Glen, from end to end and side to side, was clothed in a glistering mantle white as no fuller on earth could white it, that flung its skirts over the clumps of trees and scattered farm-houses, and was only divided where the Tochty ran with black, swollen stream. The great moor rose and fell in swelling billows of snow that arched themselves over the burns, running deep in the mossy ground, and hid the black peat bogs with a thin, treacherous crust. Beyond, the hills northwards and westwards stood high in white majesty, save where the black crags of Glen Urtach broke the line, and, above our lower Grampians, we caught glimpses of the distant peaks that lifted their heads in holiness unto God

It seemed to me a fitting day for William MacLure's funeral, rather than summer time, with its flowers and golden corn. He had not been a soft man, nor had he lived an easy life, and now he was to be laid to rest amid the austere majesty of winter, yet in the shining of the sun. Jamie Soutar, with whom I toiled across the Glen, did not think with me, but was gravely concerned.

"Nae doot it's a grand sicht; the like o't is no gien tae us twice in a generation, an' nae king wes ever carried tae his tomb in sic a cathedral.

"But it's the fouk a'm conseederin', an' hoo they 'ill win through; it's hard eneuch for them 'at's on the road, an' it's clean impossible for the lave.

"They 'ill dae their best, every man o' them, ye may depend on that, an' hed it been open weather there wudna hev been six able-bodied men missin'.

"A' wes mad at them, because they never said onything when he was leevin', but they felt for a' that what he hed dune, an', a' think, he kent it afore he deed.

"He hed juist ae faut, tae ma thinkin', for a' never jidged the waur o' him for his titch of rochness—guid trees hae gnarled bark—but he thocht ower little o' himsel.

"Noo, gin a' hed asked him hoo mony fouk wud come tae his beerial, he wud hae said, 'They 'ill be Drumsheugh an' yersel', an' maybe twa or three neeburs besides the minister,' an' the fact is that nae man in oor time wud hae sic a githerin' if it werena for the storm.

"Ye see," said Jamie, who had been counting heads all morning, there's six shepherds in Glen Urtach—they're shut up fast; an' there micht hae been a gude half dizen frae Dunleith wy, an' a'm telt there's nae road; an' there's the heich Glen, nae man cud cross the muir the day, an' it's aucht mile round;" and Jamie proceeded to review the Glen in every detail of age, driftiness of road and strength of body, till we arrived at the doctor's cottage, when he had settled on a reduction of fifty through stress of weather.

Drumsheugh was acknowledged as chief mourner by the Glen, and received us at the gate with a laboured attempt at everyday manners.

"Ye've hed heavy traivellin', a' doot, an' ye 'ill be cauld. It's hard weather for the sheep, an' a'm thinkin' this 'ill be a feeding storm.

"There wes nae use trying tae dig oot the front door yestreen, for it wud hae been drifted up again before morning. We've cleared awa the snow at the back for the prayer; ye 'ill get in at the kitchen door.

"There's a puckle Dunleith men——"

"Wha?" cried Jamie in an instant.

"Dunleith men," said Drumsheugh.

"Div ye mean they're here, whar are they?"

"Drying themsels at the fire, an' no withoot need; ane of them gied ower the head in a drift, and his neeburs hed tae pu' him oot.

"It took them a gude fower oors tae get across, an' it wes coorse wark;

they likit him weel doon that wy, an', Jamie man"—here Drumsheugh's voice changed its note, and his public manner disappeared—"what div ye think o' this? every man o' them hes on his blacks."

"It's mair than cud be expeckit," said Jamie; "but what dae yon men come frae, Drumsheugh?"

Two men in plaids were descending the hill behind the doctor's cottage, taking three feet at a stride, and carrying long staffs in their hands.

"They're Glen Urtach men, Jamie, for ane o' them wes at Kildrummie fair wi' sheep, but hoo they've wun doon passes me."

"It canna be, Drumsheugh," said Jamie, greatly excited. "Glen Urtach's steikit up wi' sna like a locked door."

"Ye're no surely frae the Glen, lads?" as the men leaped the dyke and crossed to the back door, the snow falling from their plaids as they walked.

"We're that an' no mistak, but a' thocht we wud be likit ae place, eh, Chairlie? a'm no sae weel acquaint wi' the hill on this side, an' a'm gled ye're safe."

"He cam through as bad himself tae help ma wife," was Charlie's reply.

"They're three mair Urtach shepherds 'ill come in by sune; the're frae Upper Urtach, an' we saw them fording the river; ma certes, it took them a' their time, for it wes up tae their waists and rinnin' like a mill lade, but they jined hands and cam ower fine." And the Urtach men went in to the fire.

The Glen began to arrive in twos and threes, and Jamie, from a point of vantage at the gate, and under an appearance of utter indifference, checked his roll till even he was satisfied.

"Weelum MacLure 'ill hae the beerial he deserves in spite o' sna and drifts; it passes a' tae see hoo they've githered frae far an' near."

"A'm thinkin' ye can colleck them for the minister noo, Drumsheugh. A'body's here except the heich Glen, an' we mauna luke for them."

"Dinna be sae sure o' that, Jamie. Yon's terrible like them on the road, wi' Whinnie at their heads;" and so it was, twelve in all, only old Adam Ross absent, detained by force, being eighty-two years of age.

"It wud hae been temptin' Providence tae cross the muir," Whinnie explained, "and it's a fell stap roond; a' doot we're laist."

"See, Jamie," said Drumsheugh, as he went to the house, "gin there be ony antern body in sicht afore we begin; we maun mak allooances the day wi' twa feet o' sna on the grund, tae say naethin' o' drifts."

"There's something at the turnin', an' it's no fouk; it's a machine o' some kind or ither—maybe a bread cart that's focht its wy up."

"Na, it's no that; there's twa horses, ane afore the ither; if it's no a dogcairt wi' twa men in the front; they 'ill be comin' tae the beerial."

"What wud ye sae, Jamie," Hillocks suggested, "but it micht be some o' thae Muirtown doctors? they were awfu' chief wi' MacLure."

"It's nae Muirtown doctors," cried Jamie, in great exultation, "nor ony ither doctors. A' ken thae horses, and wha's ahint them. Quick, man Hillocks, stop the fouk, and tell Drumsheugh tae come oot, for Lord Kilspindie hes come up frae Muirtown Castle."

Jamie himself slipped behind, and did not wish to be seen.

"It's the respeck he's getting' the day frae high an' low," was Jamie's husky apology; "tae think o' them fechtin' their wy doon frae Glen Urtach, and toiling roond frae the heich Glen, an' his lordship driving through the drifts a' the road frae Muirtown, juist tae honour Weelum MacLure's beerial.

"It's nae ceremony the day, ye may lippen tae it; it's the hert brocht the fouk, an' ye can see it in their faces; ilka man hes his ain reason, an' he's thinkin' on't, though he's speakin' o' naethin' but the storm; he's mindin' the day Weelum pued him oot frae the jaws o' death, or the nicht he savit the gude wife in her oor o' tribble.

"That's why they pit on their blacks this mornin' afore it wes licht, and wrestled through the sna drifts at risk o' life. Drumtochty fouk canna say muckle, it's an awfu' peety, and they 'ill dae their best tae show naethin', but a' can read it a' in their een.

"But wae's me"—and Jamie broke down utterly behind a fir tree, so tender a thing is a cynic's heart—"that fouk 'ill tak a man's best wark a' his days withoot a word an' no dae him honour till he dees. Oh, if they hed only gathered like this juist aince when he wes livin', an' lat him see he hedna laboured in vain. His reward hes come ower late, ower late."

During Jamie's vain regret, the Castle trap, bearing the marks of a wild passage in the snow-covered wheels, a broken shaft tied with rope, a twisted lamp, and the panting horses, pulled up between two rows of farmers, and Drumsheugh received his lordship with evident emotion.

"Ma lord...we never thocht o' this...an' sic a rod."

"How are you, Drumsheugh? and how are you all this wintry day?

"That's how I'm half an hour late; it took us four hour's stiff work for sixteen miles, mostly in the drifts, of course."

"It wes gude o' yir lordship, tae mak sic an effort, an' the hale Glen wull be gratefu' tae ye, for ony kindness tae him is kindness tae us."

"You make too much of it, Drumsheugh," and the clear, firm voice was heard of all; "it would have taken more than a few snow drifts to keep me from showing my respect to William MacLure's memory."

When all had gathered in a half circle before the kitchen door, Lord Kilspindie came out—every man noticed he had left his overcoat, and was in black, like the Glen—and took a place in the middle with Drumsheugh and Burnbrae, his two chief tenants, on the right and left, and as the minister appeared every man bared his head.

The doctor looked on the company—a hundred men such as for strength and gravity you could hardly have matched in Scotland—standing out in picturesque relief against the white background, and he said:

"It's a bitter day, friends, and some of you are old; perhaps it might be wise to cover your heads before I begin to pray."

Lord Kilspindie, standing erect and grey-headed between the two oldest men, replied:

"We thank you, Dr. Davidson, for your thoughtfulness; but he endured many a storm in our service, and we are not afraid of a few minutes' cold at his funeral."

A look flashed round the stern faces, and was reflected from the minister, who seemed to stand higher.

His prayer, we noticed with critical appreciation, was composed for the occasion, and the first part was a thanksgiving to God for the life-work of our doctor, wherein each clause was a reference to his services and sacrifices. No one moved or said Amen—it had been strange with us—but when every man had heard the gratitude of his dumb heart offered to Heaven, there was a great sigh.

After which the minister prayed that we might have grace to live as this man had done from youth to old age, not for himself, but for others, and that we might be followed to our grave by somewhat of "that love wherewith we mourn this day Thy servant departed." Again the same sigh, and the minister said Amen.

The "wricht" stood in the doorway without speaking, and four stalwart men came forward. They were the volunteers that would lift the coffin and carry it for the first stage. One was Tammas, Annie Mitchell's man; and another was Saunders Baxter, for whose life MacLure had his great fight with death; and the third was the Glen Urtach shepherd for whose wife's sake MacLure suffered a broken leg and three fractured ribs in a drift; and the fourth, a Dunleith man, had his own reasons of remembrance.

"He's far lichter then ye wud expeck for sae big a man—there wesna muckle left o' him, ye see—but the road is heavy, and a'll change ye aifter the first half mile."

"Ye needna tribble yersel, wricht," said the man from Glen Urtach; "the'll be nae change in the cairryin' the day," and Tammas was thankful someone had saved him from speaking.

Surely no funeral is like unto that of a doctor for pathos, and a peculiar sadness fell on that company as his body was carried out who for nearly half a century had been their help in sickness, and had beaten back death time after time from their door. Death after all was victor, for the man that saved them had not been able to save himself.

As the coffin passed the stable door a horse neighed within, and every man looked at his neighbour. It was his old mare crying to her master.

Jamie slipped into the stable, and went up into the stall.

"Puir lass, ye're no gaein' wi' him the day, an' ye 'ill never see him again; ye've hed yir last ride thegither, an' ye were true tae the end."

After the funeral Drumsheugh came himself for Jess, and took her to his farm. Saunders made a bed for her with soft, dry straw, and prepared for her supper such things as horses love. Jess would neither take food nor rest, but moved uneasily in her stall, and seemed to be waiting for someone that never came. No man knows what a horse or a dog understands and feels, for God hath not given them our speech. If any footstep was heard in the courtyard, she began to neigh, and was always looking round as the door opened. But nothing would tempt her to eat, and in the night-time Drumsheugh heard her crying as if she expected to be taken out for some sudden journey. The Kildrummie veterinary came to see her, and said that nothing could be done when it happened after this fashion with an old horse.

"A've seen it aince afore," he said. "Gin she were a Christian instead o' a horse, ye micht say she wes dying o' a broken hert."

He recommended that she should be shot to end her misery, but no man could be found in the Glen to do the deed, and Jess relieved them of the trouble. When Drumsheugh went to the stable on Monday morning, a week after Dr. MacLure fell on sleep, Jess was resting at last, but her eyes were open and her face turned to the door.

"She wes a' the wife he hed," said Jamie, as he rejoined the procession, "an' they luved ane anither weel."

The black thread wound itself along the whiteness of the Glen, the coffin first, with his lordship and Drumsheugh behind, and the others as they pleased, but in closer ranks than usual, because the snow on either side was deep, and because this was not as other funerals. They could see the women standing at the door of every house on the hillside, and weeping, for each family had some good reason in forty years to remember MacLure. When Bell Baxter saw Saunders alive, and the coffin of the doctor that saved him on her man's shoulder, she bowed her head on the dyke, and the bairns in the village made such a wail for him they that the men nearly disgraced themselves.

"A'm gled we're through that, at ony rate," said Hillocks; "he wes awfu' taen up wi' the bairns, conseederin' he hed nane o' his ain."

There was only one drift on the road between his cottage and the kirkyard, and it had been cut early that morning.

Before daybreak Saunders had roused the lads in the bothy, and they had set to work by the light of lanterns with such good will that, when Drumsheugh came down to engineer a circuit for the funeral, there was a fair passage, with walls of snow twelve feet high on either side.

"Man, Saunders," he said, "this wes a kind thocht, and rael weel dune."

But Saunders' only reply was this:

"Mony a time he's hed tae gang roond: he micht as weel hae an open road for his last traivel."

When the coffin was laid down at the mouth of the grave, the only blackness in the white kirkyard, Tammas Mitchell did the most beautiful thing in all his life. He knelt down and carefully wiped off the snow the wind had blown upon the coffin, and which had covered the name, and when he had done this he disappeared behind the others, so that Drumsheugh could hardly find him to take a cord. For these were the eight that buried Dr. MacLure—Lord Kilspindie at the head as landlord and Drumsheugh at the feet as his friend; the two ministers of the parish came first on the right and left; then Burnbrae and Hillocks of the farmers, and Saunders and Tammas for the ploughmen. So the Glen he loved laid him to rest.

When the bedrel had finished his work and the turf had been spread, Lord Kilspindie spoke:

"Friends of Drumtochty, it would not be right that we should part in silence and no man say what is in every heart. We have buried the remains of one that served this Glen with a devotion that has known no reserve, and a kindliness that never failed, for more than forty years. I have seen many brave men in my day, but no man in the trenches of Sebastopol carried himself more knightly than William MacLure. You will never have heard from his lips what I may tell you today, that my father secured for him a valuable post in his younger days, and he preferred to work among his own people; and I wished to do many things for him when he was old, but he would have nothing for himself. He will never be forgotten while one of us lives, and I pray that all doctors everywhere may share his spirit. If it be your pleasure, I shall erect a cross above his grave, and shall ask my old friend and companion Dr. Davidson, your minister, to choose the text to be inscribed."

"We thank you, Lord Kilspindie," said the doctor, "for your presence with us in our sorrow and your tribute to the memory of William MacLure, and I choose this for his text:

'Greater love hath no man than this, that a man lay down his life for his friends.'"

Milton was, at that time, held in the bonds of a very bitter theology, and his indignation was stirred by this unqualified eulogium.

"No doubt Dr. MacLure hed mony natural virtues, an' he did his wark weel, but it wes a peety he didna mak mair profession o' releegion."

"When William MacLure appears before the Judge, Milton," said Lachlan Campbell, who that day spoke his last words in public, and they were in defence of charity, "He will not be asking him about is professions, for the doctor's judgment hass been ready long ago; and it iss a good judgment, and you and I will be happy men if we get the like of it.

"It iss written in the Gospel, but it iss William MacLure that will not be expecting it."

"What is't, Lachlan?" asked Jamie Soutar, eagerly.

The old man, now very feeble, stood in the middle of the road, and his face, once so hard, was softened into a winsome tenderness.

'Come, ye blessed of My Father...I was sick, and ye visited Me.' "

A Brief History of the Edinburgh School of Medicine

JOHN RAFFENSPERGER, M.D.

THIS BRIEF HISTORICAL REVIEW PUTS "RAB" AND "A Doctor of the Old School" into an historical perspective of the Edinburgh School. The surgical history of Edinburgh begins with incorporation of the barber surgeons as craftsmen in 1508. At the end of the sixteenth century, an apprenticeship of six years was required to become an assistant surgeon. The barber surgeons constructed a guild hall with a theater for public dissection of bodies to study anatomy in 1697. The barbers and surgeons separated in 1718. In 1778 King George III signed an act which created the Royal College of Surgeons of Edinburgh. In 1681, the town council appointed three physicians as professors of medicine at the university. The Edinburgh method, which combined a university education in humanities and natural science with the clinical study of patients in a hospital, can be traced to the University of Leiden in Holland. Archibald Pitcairne was an Edinburgh physician who became a professor of physics at Leiden in 1692. Pitcairne soon returned to Edinburgh and with John Munro founded the medical school. In 1697, the College of Surgeons erected a new hall and an anatomical theater where Munro taught anatomy, a practice carried out by his son and grandson.

Herman Boerhaave, the professor of medicine at Leiden between 1709 and 1738, was the real spark behind the Edinburgh School. There was close trade between Edinburgh and Holland across the North Sea as Scottish Presbyterians sought religious asylum in Holland. Many Scottish students were influenced by Boerhaave. This remarkable genius held a degree in philosophy and had deep interests in mathematics, botany, chemistry and clinical medicine. He was fluent in German, French, English and Latin. Between 1701 and his death in 1738, Boerhaave was first a lecturer on the institutes of medicine and he then held the chairs of chemistry, botany, and medicine. He was a brilliant teacher who attracted students from all over the world. In Leiden, there was a well equipped medical school, chemical laboratories, a fine botanical garden and an extensive library. Boerhaave's great genius was his ability to teach students the importance of symptoms and the accurate observation of physical signs at the bedside of a sick patient. It seems impossible to believe that bedside teaching was not generally given to medical students until the end of the nineteenth century. Most doctors learned by attending a series of lectures.

Fueled by the example of Boerhaave, Scottish physicians returned to Edinburgh determined to carry on the medical school founded by Pitcairne and John Munroe. One of these students, Alexander Munro, the son of John, studied first with his father, then in London, Paris, and finally in Leiden. He was appointed professor of anatomy and surgery by the Town Council in 1720 at the age of 22. John and Alexander Munro were instrumental in founding the Royal Edinburgh Infirmary in 1729, providing a hospital for the poor as well as a place for medical students to learn clinical medicine. Other Scottish physicians who had studied at Leiden returned to teach in the new school.

One physician, John Rutherford, began a course of lectures in practical medicine at the Royal Infirmary. Sir William Osler said of the Rutherford lectures, "They are of great value as a record of clinical teaching in the English-speaking schools and what has been called the Edinburgh method dates from the introductions of Rutherford's practical classes in the Royal Infirmary." Alexander Munro's son and grandson, (primus, secundus, and tertious) continued to teach anatomy through the 1700s. By 1765, the fame of the Edinburgh School had spread and students came to it as they had to Leiden a generation before. Between 1726 and 1799, one-hundred and ninety-five students came from North America alone. Benjamin Rush who signed the Declaration of Independence and Casper Wistar and Phylip Syng Physic who founded the first medical school in the United States at the University of Pennsylvania, were Edinburgh graduates.

While the Munroes were the leading anatomists and teachers in the medical school, they were not surgeons. During the latter portion of the eighteenth century, Benjamin Rush and then John Bell were the leading surgeons in Edinburgh. They lectured on diseases commonly contracted due to surgery, and when the opportunity arose they would operate before medical students. One of the American students who studied with John Bell in 1793-94 was Ephraim McDowell. At that time, before anesthesia or antisepsis, no surgeon had ever successfully opened the peritoneal cavity to remove an ovarian tumor. However, during a lecture on diseases of the ovaries, John Bell suggested that such an operation might be possible. McDowell carried out his teacher's suggestion and became the first to successfully remove an ovarian tumor. This historic operation was carried out in Danville, Kentucky, in 1809, on a frontier woman who survived for many years after her operation. McDowell went on to become one of the leading surgeons west of Philadelphia. The operation pioneered by McDowell was later adopted by Scottish surgeons. It is quite possible that this was the operation performed by Sir George on Annie Mitchell.

In addition to teaching medical students, surgeons required bodies to practice operations, so that when they worked upon living patients they could operate with greater dexterity. Although the bodies of executed criminals and unwanted orphans were used for anatomical dissection, a considerable number of bodies were sold to medical schools by grave robbers. There were complaints of violations of graves in Greyfriar's churchyard as early as 1711. The usual practice was to open the head of a grave, pull the corpse out of its casket, and then place the body in a bag. The grave robbers stole away in the night to sell the body.

The last Munro at the medical school was not a particularly inspired teacher; he used his grandfather's notes and mumbled his lectures. As a result, in the early 1800s there appeared several "extramural" anatomy teachers who gave lectures which included anatomic demonstrations and were given for university credit. There was for awhile two rival teachers, John Barclay and Robert Knox. Knox was the more dramatic and consequently attracted the most students.

The increased demand for anatomical material led to more grave robbing until two body snatchers, or "resurrectionists," William Hare and his accomplice Burke, decided it would be simpler to secure bodies by intoxicating and then strangling inmates of their boardinghouse. They suffocated at least sixteen victims, some of whom were found in Robert Knox's dissection rooms. The subsequent public clamor resulted in the retirement of Knox from Edinburgh, despite the support of his students.

The infamous case of Burke and Hare that led to the retirement of Knox left the teaching of anatomy and surgery to his rival John Barclay. This appointment led to the succession of Robert Liston, James Syme, and Joseph Lister, the three surgeons who dominated surgery in Edinburgh for fifty years.

Robert Liston was born in 1794 and studied the classics and mathematics at the University of Edinburgh before he joined John Barclay to study medicine. By 1815, he was an assistant and prosector for Barclay as well as a house surgeon at the Royal Infirmary. He also studied surgery in London for a year and passed the examination for the Royal College of Surgeons of both London and Edinburgh.

Liston was the most brilliant surgeon of his time. He could rapidly amputate a thigh with one hand while he applied pressure to the femoral artery with the other. He wrote extensively and advocated rapid operations and the placing of the skin on a stretch during the initial incision to reduce pain. Liston became Surgeon to the Royal Infirmary in 1828, but five years later went to the North London Hospital as Professor of Clinical Surgery. In his textbook of practical surgery, Liston described amputations, fractures, rectal prolapse, bladder stones, hernias, and most of the diseases which could be diagnosed on the surface of the body. Though quarrelsome with his associates, he was kind and considerate to his patients. He was the first surgeon in England to use ether, only five days after news of the new anesthetic agent reached Britain from the United States.

James Syme, born in 1799, attended Edinburgh University and became Liston's assistant in 1818. In 1823, Liston gave up teaching and Syme took over his students. He gave lectures, conducted anatomical demonstrations, and performed operations. This provided Syme with great experience, helping him become as skilled as Liston. Unfortunately, the two men quarreled when Liston was the Chief Surgeon at the Royal Infirmary. Thus, Syme was denied an appointment at the infirmary and had nowhere to practice.

He opened his own surgical hospital in a mansion, the Minto House, in May of 1828. This was the same year that Burke was executed for killing his victims and selling the bodies to Robert Knox. Syme then attracted many students who paid him to teach anatomy and surgery. Minto House, which had 24 patient beds and a large, well-lit operating room, was busy and successful. Syme's practice grew so large that he required three assistants during the four years he operated at Minto House.

John Brown, the author of "Rab," the third assistant to Syme, became his lifelong friend and companion. The operation upon Ailie, described in "Rab," took place at Minto House in December 1830. The story, however, was not published until 1858. Syme clearly understood the pathology and prognosis of breast cancer and he described mastectomy in his "Principles of Surgery," published in 1832. Unlike other operations which could be performed rapidly to reduce pain, a mastectomy for cancer was done with painstaking care in order to remove the tumor along with involved axillary lymph nodes. He recognized that a permanent cure could be achieved if there was no invasion of the muscle and if involved axillary glands could be removed.

The students described in "Rab" who saw Ailie's operation were awed by the fortitude of the patient. However, some medical students were so repulsed by the pain and agony inflicted upon patients during surgery that they gave up medicine. One was Charles Darwin, who fled from the operating room and didn't return. Another was James Simpson, who ran away from a breast amputation performed by Liston during the same period. He planned to give up medicine, but instead resolved to find some means to make operations less painful. He later discovered and popularized the anesthetic properties of chloroform, which was easier to use and produced fewer side effects than ether.

Chloroform was first used at the Royal Infirmary on a five year old boy with osteomyelitis of the radius. The operation performed by Syme on Ailie is perhaps the most graphic description in the English language of an operation performed prior to anesthesia. The fact that it so moved John Brown, as well as the other students who witnessed the operation, is an index to the compassion for suffering that these physicians had for their patients.

When Robert Liston went to London, James Syme became Surgeon-in-Chief at the Royal Infirmary in 1833. He held this position until 1869, when Joseph Lister, his son-in-law, succeeded him. Syme was an innovative and dedicated surgeon who attracted patients from all over Scotland. Even before the introduction of anesthesia, he performed many complex operations, including an extensive jaw resection for a tumor, nasal reconstructions, joint excisions and the forefoot amputation which still bears his name.

He also wrote extensively and carried out research on the regeneration of bone from periosteum. After the introduction of anesthesia, the numbers of surgical operations increased dramatically, so much that Syme insisted on the construction of an entire surgical hospital of one hundred-ninety beds at the Royal Infirmary, which was opened in 1853.

James Syme may well be our first modern surgeon. He was well grounded in anatomy, the only surgical basic science of the time. He recognized the necessity of conserving blood during an operation and it was said of him that he never wasted a drop of blood or a word. He was a teacher who inspired medical students and young surgeons alike. He carried out original research and authored textbooks of surgery. His career as Surgeon-in-Chief to the Royal Infirmary lasted for thirty-six years. During this time he was often at odds with the hospital administrators, a trait which continues in modern day surgeons.

Throughout his life, Syme had an active, inquiring mind. He adapted the use of anesthesia and antisepsis as soon as their discoveries became known. This is to his great credit, since many of his contemporaries vigorously opposed the discoveries of Lister. Syme died with a lingering illness shortly after he retired as Surgeon-in-Chief in 1869. His friend, John Brown, continued to visit him to the end. Perhaps his most enduring and important quality was described in "Rab": "he was a kind surgeon."

Joseph Lister visited Edinburgh to observe Syme at work in 1843, the same year which saw the opening of the new surgical hospital. He was twenty-six years old when he arrived in Scotland. He had graduated with a Bachelor's of Medicine from the University College Hospital in London and had already passed his examination for the Royal College of Surgeons. He had originally planned to study surgery on the Continent, but his teachers in London advised him to visit Syme in Edinburgh.

Lister found at the Royal Infirmary superior surgical facilities with an unrivaled opportunity to study disease. Furthermore, the large body of students stimulated an exchange of ideas and study. Syme had a highly organized surgical department where all types of cases could be observed, studied, and operated upon. Syme received Lister with great warmth and almost immediately made him one of his assistants. A year later, Lister married Syme's daughter and secured a position at the Royal Infirmary as an attending surgeon. He also gave a series of lectures to the medical students at the University.

From the very beginning of his work in Edinburgh, Lister worked on the problem of surgical infection. Complications such as sepsis, tetanus, blood poisoning, gangrene, erysipelas and secondary hemorrhage almost invariably occurred following surgical operations or trauma. There was a 43 percent mortality rate following amputation in Edinburgh, but elsewhere as many as 75 to 90 percent of patients died following major limb amputations.

A few surgeons realized that cleanliness helped reduce the incidence of infection, but no one understood the role of bacteria. Lister conducted endless researches and finally made the connection between fermentation and suppuration. Certainly, the intellectual atmosphere of Edinburgh stimulated him to solve the problem of surgical infection. Perhaps it is no coincidence that the story of "Rab and his Friends" was published in 1858 while Lister was in Edinburgh, and that the author, John Brown, was his friend.

The concept of a "house surgeon," or resident, came about while Syme worked with Lister at the Royal Infirmary, in the mid-seventeenth century. This was the forerunner of the system which did not become important in surgical education in this country until Halstead instituted it at John Hopkins in the early 1900s. One of the house surgeons who worked with Syme and Lister was Joseph Bell, who became the model for Sherlock Holmes in Conan Doyle's detective novels. It's clear that these doctors, in addition to their enduring qualities of compassion and intellect, were also privileged to work, together, with some of the foremost surgeons of their time because of the stimulating environment they promoted.

In 1860, Lister was appointed to the Chair of Surgery at Glasgow. There, on August 12, 1865, his work and studies bore fruit. Lister had decided that a chemical could be used to prevent putrefaction. He chose carbolic acid, because of its efficacy in the treatment of sewage. His patient was an eleven-year old boy with a compound fracture of the tibia. Ordinarily, this sort of case would have been treated with amputation. Instead, Lister applied undiluted carbolic acid to the wound, which healed without infection. In 1867, Lister reported on eleven cases of compound fractures similarly treated with only one death.

Lister was appointed Professor of Clinical Surgery in Edinburgh to succeed Syme in 1869. Syme had built the most prestigious surgical department in the world. He himself had taken up the antiseptic technique and had reported his results in 1868. When Syme's health failed, there was little doubt that Lister would return to assume the Chair of Surgery. Lister had many friends in Edinburgh. John Brown was among the first to write a note of congratulations to Lister on his new appointment.

Upon his return to Edinburgh, Lister continued his work on the antiseptic technique and attracted large numbers of patients and students.

He made teaching rounds in the hospital, performed operations, carried out research, and taught countless surgeons from all over the world. It is difficult to understand why so many surgeons, among them men who worked in the same hospital with Lister, refused to believe in his methods. Clearly his surgical results were far superior to those who did not adopt the antiseptic technique. But both surgeons and physicians scoffed at bacteria, which they could not see. Even though surgeons were reluctant to accept the germ theory, students and patients enthusiastically flocked to Lister's clinic.

One of them, the poet William Ernest Henley, spent twenty months (from 1873–1875) on Lister's surgical service at the Royal Infirmary and left a legacy of poetry which describes the hospital and the conditions of the day. Henley's left foot had already been amputated for tuberculous arthritis. When his right foot became diseased, surgeons in England advised another amputation. Henley refused and instead journeyed to Edinburgh where he heard that Lister was excising infected joints with the antiseptic method, avoiding amputation.

The surgical hospital where Henley was a patient was heated by open fireplaces and there was no running water or plumbing facilities. Henley's poems describe the grim, dingy waiting rooms, his fellow patients, the nurses, house surgeons, Lister himself, and the long days and nights of languishing in bed.

OPERATION

You are carried in a basket
Like a carcass from the shambles,
To the Theatre, a cockpit
Where they stretch you on a table.
Then they bid you close your eyelids
And they mask you with a napkin,
And the anesthetic reaches
Hot and subtle through your being.

And you grasp and reel and shudder
In a rushing, swaying rapture,

While the voices at your elbow
Fade—receding—fainter—farther.

Lights about you shower and tumble,
And your blood seems crystallizing—
Edged and vibrant, yet within you
Racked and hurried back and forward.

Then the lights grow fast and furious,
And you hear a noise of waters,
And you wrestle, blind and dizzy,
In an agony of effort.
Till a sudden lull accepts you,
And you sound an utter darkness...
        And awaken...with a struggle...
        On a hushed, attentive audience.

Henley became a close friend of Robert Lewis Stevenson while he was a patient at the Royal Infirmary and was the model for Long John Silver in *Treasure Island*.

Lister continued his research, experimenting with various types of suture, drainage tubes and new techniques, including the wiring of a fractured patella. Lister traveled in the United States during 1876, espousing his methods, but he received a cool reception, because surgeons continued to see the germ theory as a myth. He left Edinburgh to become the Surgeon at King's College in London in 1877, principally to convince English surgeons of his work. Eventually his persistence and excellent results won over the medical profession. We can thank Lister for the fact that today, a patient can undergo an extensive operation with minimal risk of developing an infection in the wound.

Lister's greatest trait was his invariable gentleness and sympathy. He seldom referred to a patient as a "case" but introduced his remarks with such kindly terms as "this poor fellow" or "this little child." Once a small urchin in the wards, as his eyes followed Lister's movements, confided to a bystander, "It's us wee yins he likes best, and next it's the auld women."

For all his humbleness of spirit, Lister was the surgeon summoned to treat Queen Victoria when she developed an axillary abscess, and interestingly enough, it was his failure to attain sufficient drainage with a wick of gauze which led Lister to use, for the first time, a rubber drainage tube.

For Lister's work, he was made a Baronet in 1883 and a Lord in 1897. In London there is a public monument in his honor which bears a single word, "LISTER."

The surgeon who succeeded Lister to the Chair of Surgery at the University of Glasgow in 1869 was Sir George H. Macleod, another Scottish doctor whose father was a distinguished Presbyterian minister. He had graduated from the University of Glasgow and in 1854 went to the Crimean War. He was the senior surgeon at a civil hospital in Smyrna and then managed to obtain an appointment in a front line hospital where he worked under fire. Doctor Macleod wrote a number of articles on the treatment of gunshot wounds and did a great deal to improve the care of the wounded. He returned to Glasgow to become a distinguished surgeon, teacher, and an outstanding public speaker.

Since he was a surgeon at the Royal Infirmary, he would have been among the first to know of Lister's work with antisepsis. Macleod was the "Sir George" who came by train to Drumtochty, forded the flooded river with Doctor MacLure, and operated upon Annie Mitchell. According to a review of "A Doctor of the Old School," which appeared in the *Lancet*, the operation was a laparotomy. The influence of Lister was there because Sir George's last words were "mind the antiseptic dressings." Not only did he utilize the most modern surgical techniques, but he is an example of the compassion and kindliness which distinguished the Scottish surgeons. Sir George Macleod had every honor, he was well-to-do, busy with a large practice, and had teaching responsibilities, yet he took time to journey to a remote highland village to operate on a poor farmer's wife. When he learned how Dr. MacLure and his friend, Drumsheugh, had used their own money for his fee, he tore up the check.

JOHN BROWN (1810–1882), the author of "Rab," is the key person in our narrative because he was not only a kind and compassionate physician, but he was also a gifted writer. Both his father and grandfather were ministers in the United Presbyterian Church, a background shared by a number of Scottish physicians. He was born in 1810 and moved to Edinburgh when he was eleven years old. Bob Ainslie, mentioned in "Rab," was his friend while he attended the public high school. He then went to the University of Edinburgh and became an apprentice to James Syme at the Minto House Hospital. The events in "Rab" took place in 1830, when he was still only twenty years old. In his preface to the first edition of *Horae Subsecivae,* Doctor Brown said concerning "Rab" and his association with Syme,

> I have no apologies for bringing in "Rab and His Friends" I did so remembering well the good I got then, as a man and a doctor. It let me see down into the depths of our common nature and feel the strong and gentle touch that we all need, and never forget, which makes the whole world kin; and it gave me an opportunity of introducing in a way which he cannot dislike, for he knows it is true, my old master and friend, Professor Syme, whose indenture I am thankful to possess.

Although John Brown was fascinated with surgery, he was more interested in literature. After his apprenticeship with Syme, he apprenticed to a general practitioner in Chatham and, in 1833, returned to Edinburgh to establish his practice. While in Chatham, he was one of two physicians who stayed with their patients during a cholera epidemic. During one of his last visits to Scotland, Charles Dickens remembered the incident and congratulated Doctor Brown on his courage for staying with his patients during the epidemic.

Doctor Brown had a comfortable practice which allowed him to pursue his many other interests which included children, literature, poetry, art, nature, and dog breeding. He first published his *Horae Subsecivae*, which roughly translates into *Idle Hours*, in 1858. This was a collection of observations and short stories (including "Rab") which he had written over the years. It was an immediate success. His next most popular work, "Marjorie Fleming," a story about a precocious child who was a great friend of Sir Walter Scott, also achieved immediate acclaim.

He wrote a number of other short stories and articles for general readers, including five sermons on health addressed to working people. These essays emphasized cleanliness, good food, and moderation in drink, rest, and other habits which would ward off sickness. On the one hand, he defined the duties of the physician to cure and be kind to his patients, to tell his patients the truth and keep their secrets. Today's physicians could find no better advice! He advises patients to trust and obey their doctors and to be truthful when describing their symptoms. Furthermore, the patient has a duty to reward the doctor, not only with money, but with gratitude and by speaking well of him. He rated gratitude above financial reward, and I believe this is still true of most modern doctors.

He carried on an extensive correspondence with Carlyle, Ruskin, Thackeray, Oliver Wendell Holmes, and Samuel Clemens, as well as with his friends. We gain some measure of the affection and respect which John Brown's associates held for him by quoting the following description by his sister, "Brother John was a doctor whom everybody liked, his quick sympathy was truly personal in every case. In 'Rab' he saw something that others did not see."

Sir William Osler caught the essence of John Brown and *Horae Subsecivae* in a review of the third volume for the *Medical News* of September 8, 1883. This was Osler's first published book review. He said that "Rab and his Friends" was now an English classic and that the keynote phrase in Brown's writings was his plea for "cultivation of and concentration of the unassisted senses" in diagnosis. He called Brown an exuberant classical scholar whose quotations from Latin, Greek, and the older English classics overflow on almost every page. It is pure speculation, but I would like to think that the reading of "Rab and His Friends" influenced Osler to become a physician, rather than a clergyman.

In recognition of his literary efforts, the University of Edinburgh gave him an honorary degree, L.L.D., in 1874. He died in 1880, alone; his wife had died before him. But he always remembered and talked about the great dog Rab, who was his companion through the years. After his death, Samuel Clemens wrote this letter to Doctor Brown's son.

> *Dear Dr. Brown,*
> *Both copies came, and we are reading and re-reading the one and lending the other to old time adorers of "Rab and His Friends." It is an exquisite book, the perfection of literary workmanship. It says so in every line. "Don't look at me, look at him," and one tries to be good and obey; but the charm of the painter is so strong that one can't keep his entire attention on the developing portrait, but must steal side glimpses of the artist, and try to devine the trick of his felicitous brush. In this book, the Doctor lives and moves just as he was.*

IAN MACLAREN (1850-1907) was the pen name of John Watson, born November 3, 1850, to a Highland family. His mother's name was Maclaren, and both his parents spoke Gaelic, and thus he had an excellent background for his stories about life in Scotland. Watson studied for the ministry at the University of Edinburgh and at Tubingen in Germany. His first ministry was in 1874 at the Parish of Logielmond in Perthshire. This experience, plus his love for the country and knowledge of crops and cattle, gave him the background for his stories about Drumtochty. His bachelor uncles provided the inspiration for Burnbrae and Drumsheugh, two of the farmers who are prominent in his stories.

After three years at Logielmond, he was appointed to the Sefton Park church in Liverpool. His earlier book, *Beside the Bonnie Brier Bush*, published in 1894, won him instant fame as a story writer. *The Days of Auld Lang Syne* and "A Doctor of the Old School" appeared the following year. As a result of these books and other stories, he became recognized as one of the best interpreters of life in the Highlands and of the Scottish character. He was tall, athletic and a brilliant public speaker. It was his skill as a speaker which brought him increased fame and recognition in the United States.

He toured the U.S. in the fall of 1896, beginning at Yale, where he delivered the Lyman Beecher Lectures on Preaching and was given an honorary Doctor of Divinity degree. His public speaking tour was a tremendous success, enrapturing large sophisticated cities and small towns alike. A second speaking tour of the United States was equally successful, but in 1907, when he returned for the third time, his health was poor. He died of a severe attack of tonsillitis at the Iowa Wesleyan University. Doctor Watson was one of the best-loved men of his time. His portrait, painted by Robert Morrison, was hung in the Guild Room of the Sefton Park Church in Liverpool. It is now in the Liverpool Art Museum.

JOHN RAFFENSPERGER was a surgeon-in-chief at the Children's Memorial Hospital in Chicago and a professor of surgery at Northwestern University. He has authored surgical textbooks, a history of the Cook County Hospital, a collection of short stories, and a "surgical thriller." He currently lives in Sanibel Island, Florida.

BIBLIOGRAPHY

1. Bettany, G.T. *Eminent Doctors, Their Lives and Work*. London: John Hogg, 1885.
2. Brown, John. *A Biography and Criticism by the Late John Taylor Brown*. London: Adam, and Charles Black, 1903.
3. Brown, John. *Horae Subsecivae*. Edinburgh: David Douglas Co., 1832.
4. Comrie, John D. "Boerhaave and the Early Medical School at Edinburgh." *Memorialia, Hermann Boerhaave, Optimi Medici*. Haarlem: De Erven F. Bohn, N.V., 1939.
5. Comrie, John D. *History of Scottish Medicine in Two Volumes*. London: Bolliere, Tindall and Cox, 1932.
6. Coope, Robert, ed. *The Quiet Art: A Doctor's Anthology*. Edinburgh, London: E. & S Livington, Ltd., 1958.
7. Creswell, C.H. *The Royal College of Surgeons of Edinburgh, Historical Notes from 1505 to 1905*. Edinburgh: Oliver, and Boyd, 1926.
8. Downie, J.W. *The Early Physicians and Surgeons of the Western Infirmary*. Glasgow: J. Walker Downy, 1923.
9. Duttera, M. Julian, Jr. "The Healer's Hand." *Journal of the American Medical Association*. 242:41.
10. Ellis, Harold. "Lord Lister and the Compound Fracture." *Contemporary Surgery*, 15:67-68.
11. Forrest, D.W. *Letters of Dr. John Brown, With Letters from Ruskin, Thackeray and Others*. London: Adam and Charles Black, 1907.
12. Garrison, Fielding H. *An Introduction to the History of Medicine*. Philadelphia: W.B. Saunders Co., 1929.
13. Henley, William E. *Poems*. New York: Charles Scribner's Sons, 1919.
14. Liston, Robert. *Liston's Practical Surgery*. Philadelphia: Thomas Cowperthwaite & Co., 1842.
15. Mill, S.T. *Dr. John Brown and His Sister Isabella*. Edinburgh: David Douglas, 1889.

16. Nicoll, W. Robertson. *The Life of Rev. John Watson D.D.* London: Hudder and Stoughton, 1908.

17. "Obituary Notices of Sir George Baird." *Glasgow Medical Journal.* 38: 270-27. *British Medical Journal.* 2: 637-638. *Lancet.* 2: 641.

18. Olch, Peter D. and Lloyd M. Nyhus. "Joseph Lister and the Old Edinburgh Infirmary as Described by the Poet William Ernest Henley." *Surgery, Gynecology and Obstetrics.* 112: 511-514.

19. "Our Gideon Grays. Lancet." 1: 561-562.

20. Park, Roswell. *An Epitome of the History of Medicine.* Philadelphia: F. A. Davis Co., 1903.

21. Peddie, Alexander. *Recollections of Dr. John Brown, Author of "Rab and His Friends".* London: Percival and Co., 1893.

22. Peterson, Robert. *Memorials of the Life of James Syme.* Edinburgh: Edmonton and Douglas, 1874.

23. Ridenbaugh, M.Y. *The Biography of Ephraim McDowell.* Philadelphia, 1864.

24. Simpson, Myrtle. *Simpson, The Obstetrician, A Biography.* London: Victor Gollancz Ltd., 1972.

25. Syme, James. *Contributions to the Pathology and Practice of Surgery.* Edinburgh: Edmonton and Douglas, 1862.

26. Syme James. *Observations in Classical Surgery.* Edinburgh: Edmonton and Douglas, 1862.

27. Syme, James. *The Principles of Surgery.* Edinburgh: MacLachlan and Stewart, 1832.

28. Turner, A. Logan. *Story of A Great Hospital, The Royal Infirmary of Edinburgh 1729-1929.* Edinburgh: Oliver and Boyd, 1937.

COSIMO is a specialty publisher of books and publications that inspire, inform, and engage readers. Our mission is to offer unique books to niche audiences around the world.

COSIMO BOOKS publishes books and publications for innovative authors, nonprofit organizations, and businesses.

COSIMO BOOKS specializes in bringing books back into print, publishing new books quickly and effectively, and making these publications available to readers around the world.

COSIMO CLASSICS offers a collection of distinctive titles by the great authors and thinkers throughout the ages.

At COSIMO CLASSICS timeless works find new life as affordable books, covering a variety of subjects including: Business, Economics, History, Personal Development, Philosophy, Religion & Spirituality, and much more!

COSIMO REPORTS publishes public reports that affect your world, from global trends to the economy, and from health to geopolitics.

FOR MORE INFORMATION CONTACT US AT
INFO@COSIMOBOOKS.COM

➢ if you are a book lover interested in our current catalog of books

➢ if you represent a bookstore, book club, or anyone else interested in special discounts for bulk purchases

➢ if you are an author who wants to get published

➢ if you represent an organization or business seeking to publish books and other publications for your members, donors, or customers.

COSIMO BOOKS ARE ALWAYS
AVAILABLE AT ONLINE BOOKSTORES

VISIT COSIMOBOOKS.COM
BE INSPIRED, BE INFORMED